EnlightenUp

Freeing The Real You!

Marianne T. Schorer

02 03 04 05 HH 10 9 8 7 6 5 4 3 2 1
Printed in the United States of America
ISBN: 0-9715739-2-1
Library of Congress Control #: 2002105586

Requests for permission to make copies of any part of this work can be made to:

Cameo Publications
PO Box 8006
Hilton Head Island, SC 29938

1-866-37-CAMEO
publisher@cameopublications.com
www.cameopublications.com

DEDICATION

To Clifford, my loving husband, partner and friend, for his unfailing love, affection, devotion, encouragement and support, as well as the heartfelt times filled with stimulating conversation, provocative thought, understanding, fun, and laughter.

To Dana, my daughter, for her courage, understanding, and truths.

To My Parents, for their perpetual love and support and for teaching me what it means to love from your heart.

ABOUT THE AUTHOR

MARIANNE T. SCHORER is a consultant to professionals, entrepreneurs, and corporations. Her diversified background lends objectivity and a supportive style for people to develop clear objectives coupled with definitive action plans. The result is enhanced leadership performance, creativity, and most important a comfortable balance between the pressures of daily life and a quest for inner peace.

Her techniques include building interpersonal communication skills through a series of effective exercises that strengthen both personal and business relationships. *EnlightenUP* captures the process in a concise, easy to follow program that will help as one reader commented to "finally lead me to a place of peace and happiness."

Marianne is a Certified Professional Behavioral and Values Analyst, Master Practitioner in Neuro-Linguistic Programming, and Ericksonian Hypnosis Practitioner. Her appearances on national television include O'Reilly's Fox News, Bloomberg News, and Radio. She has authored a weekly newspaper column, and is a Summa Cum Laude graduate from Manhattanville College.

Acknowledgements

Although I am responsible for writing this book, some of the ideas on which it is based are neither new nor my own. They represent the synthesis of collective knowledge and wisdom from the beginnings of time. Many colleagues and friends have shared their work and ideas with me through the years, and some of their wisdom shines forth onto the pages of this book.

First, I wish to express my deepest gratitude and appreciation to the Universal Spirit, who so knowingly and lovingly guided me through this project while providing me with an inspirational voice that paved the true direction of this book.

Second, I wish to give a sincere thanks to my spiritual teachers, Thomas Moore, Deepak Chopra, M.D., Joan Borysenko, Ph.D., Caroline Myss, Ph.D., Wayne Dyer, Ph.D., Louise Hay, Henri J. M. Nouwen, Anthony Robbins, and Stephen Covey, whose writings, audiotapes, and seminars have provided me with inspirational understandings and insights about myself and others.

Third, I would like to thank my clients, colleagues, and friends, namely Rachel Hott and Steven Leeds of the Advanced Communications Center in New York; Bill Bonnstetter, Judy Suiter, and Randy Widrick of Target Training International in Arizona; Thomas Leonard of Coach University, The Institute of Noetic Sciences; and Charlie Miller, Lionel Ketchian, Joelle Mahoney, Robert Dey, Bill Hill, and the late Miller Minor for their friendship, teachings and support.

Finally, I want to extend my deepest gratitude and appreciation to Dawn and Dave Josephson of Cameo Publications. Dawn for her extraordinary guidance, support, and encouragement. Her profound insights, talents, skills, and abilities were key in bringing this book to a new level. Dave for his exceptional cover design selection and expertise in the publication and marketing process.

Contents

EnlightenUp appeared out of the blue and for me it was a dream come true.

Our lifelong process of enlightenment encouraged me to expand my readers' wonderment at this great experience called life. In essence, I encourage you to "lighten up" and enjoy the journey.

The underlying goal of this book focuses on two main objectives, which I incorporate into the simple concept of *EnlightenUp:*

1. To help people discover, appreciate, and celebrate their uniqueness, knowing that they are born worthy and need not spend their lives proving it.
2. To help people recognize that the greatest gift they can give is the gift of themselves.

This book will help you discover your truest essence, appreciate your inherent gifts, and celebrate your life as you learn how to empower yourself and use your empowerment to help others. You will learn how to integrate your mind, body, and spirit and rely on your spirituality to enable you to heighten your humanity as you seek greater meaning in life.

The process is as simple as ABC.

- **A** is for Action and Accountability. We will create a plan focused on Action and Accountability. We will also learn how being accountable to ourselves comes before being accountable to another.
- **B** is for Being in the Flow and a Belief System. We will create a language and belief system that will enable us to live authentically and seek greater meaning, while we learn to see the world with a sense of symbolic unity.
- **C** is for Congruity and Consciousness. We will integrate our minds, bodies, and spirits and reach our authentic centers of consciousness, while relying on our spirits to transform us.

Carl Sandberg once wrote: "Nothing happens unless first a dream." The truth is that many people's dreams do not stem from conscious thoughts; rather, they evolve from expanded dimensions, directions, and paths that they never considered nor imagined possible. For me, the evolution of my dreams became a spiritual journey, a transformation that moved me from merely accepting the fact that there is a connection between all things to seeing perfection in the world around me. This understanding enabled me to heighten my own humanity and helped to spiritually enlighten me in the process.

Discovering my own spirituality revealed a path that enabled me to define and refine individual principles and beliefs that helped me understand and experience an internal sense of connection to the Universe and a Higher Power. This extraordinary journey defies scientific evidence and silently speaks of our pervasive connection to each other and to the universe as a whole. The awakening to this awe-inspiring gift of light and greatness was truly moving and overwhelming at times. It was this inspirational light that created a voice for this book.

As you begin to rely on your spirit to further integrate your mind and body, you'll seek greater meaning for your life, and you'll eventually see the world with a sense of symbolic unity. This different perspective is what will raise you to a new level of consciousness, as it serves to connect all humanity and the vast universe of which we are all a part. I invite you to join me on a "going home" journey and experience for yourself the spirituality that makes this transformation possible.

Today, self-help books are a predominant part of our culture. People buy them in droves, all with the underlying desire of wanting to feel better. This quest for personal enlightenment and growth is admirable and clearly sends a message that states, "I want to change or improve myself and my life." This statement then prompts the obvious question: "How do I do it?"

The amount of pain a person is experiencing determines the direction he or she takes. Those directions can be therapy; self-help; support of friends, family, or a coach; prayer; meditation; or self-introspection. However, these resources will take people only so far, which prompts the next question: "Where do I go from there?"

EnlightenUp suggests a combination of resources that will enhance your ability to satisfy your needs and achieve the outcome you desire in your life. Why is this so important? Quite frankly, look around. There are people with eating disorders, gambling, shopping, alcohol, or drug-related addictions. When they hit a low point and the pain begins to feel unbearable, the questions begin: "What do I do? Where do I go? How do I get help?" On a less extreme level, many people possess some sort of exercise equipment that has become a sculpture within the confines of their home. While they may have books on "how to feel healthy and be fit," many of them still sit in front of the tube and eat junk food. As their weight escalates and their self-esteem plummets, they ask the same questions as the former group: "What do I do? Where do I go? How do I get help?"

Fortunately, there are answers to these questions. However, rather than give a quick, pat answer, I want you to take a moment to think about some of your unmet needs. There is no mystery that unmet needs are generally at the root of our addictions. Think about the following questions:

- What is it that our unconscious is desperately seeking that manifests itself in a behavior of avoidance or denial of responsibility centered on fixing others rather than ourselves?

- What is it that drives us to seek other ways to ease the pain of unfulfilment when in effect we are actually sabotaging ourselves?
- What are the strong emotions brought on by our limiting beliefs and expectations, perceived threats, fears, or tolerations?

The purpose of this book is to unfold the mysteries that lurk behind the answers to the above questions. It will also take you through a process that teaches, guides, and supports you to explore a spiritual language that helps you become aware of your humanness while you discover the pathways to *EnlightenUp*. These teachings will inspire you to love, appreciate, and accept your own individuality and uniqueness. I want to stress that each person is his or her greatest asset, and each of us has the ability to draw upon the inner resources that lie within us in order to capitalize and make that asset the best it can be.

THE SPIRITUAL CONNECTION

We are all connected in a special way, and when I use the word "connection," I mean it literally. We all have various parts of ourselves that are in harmony with who we are and other parts that are not in harmony. You will learn how to understand all those parts of yourself and how to integrate them to create a life of balance, harmony, peace, love, and joy.

When you *EnlightenUp*, you experience a life of choice rather than need. You begin to shore up the internal infrastructures within yourself and then shift your focus onto the external infrastructures within your relationships. To help you do this, each chapter is specifically designed to address pivotal aspects of life. You will learn how to identify your mission, vision, values, beliefs, boundaries, and goals. You will also develop a conclusive understanding of how to formulate these aspects of your identity. In addition, you will be asked to ponder questions that elicit a response and help identify behavioral patterns. Finally, you will participate in exercises that provide you with the necessary skills, tools, techniques, and strategies that will make the process "click."

Above all else, you will begin to assimilate where you are in life compared to where you want to go, and you will develop a clear definition of "Who You Want to Be," "What Your Needs and Wants Are," and "What Other People Can and Cannot Do To You." As you journey toward self-discovery, change, and creation, you will actively go from an "unconscious place," where you are literally performing behavior and belief patterns on auto-pilot, to a "conscious level of awareness" of those patterns. At that point, the new conscious behaviors and beliefs will replace the old until they become "unconscious." I define this cycle as going from "unconscious incompetence" to "conscious incompetence" to "conscious competence" to "unconscious competence."

I'd like you to begin your journey with the following story in mind. One evening I went to a bookstore to browse. For some reason I found myself heading toward the poetry section of the store and came across a book entitled *More Treasured Poems that Touch the Heart* compiled by Mary Sanford Laurence. The book contained a variety of cherished poems and favorite poets. Among them, one poem stood out and spoke to me. It was Emily Dickinson's *If I Can Stop One Heart from Breaking*. For me, it was one of those blissful moments that clearly spoke to my heart, as it happened during a unique time when I was formulating my ideas on this book's specific mission.

> If I can stop one heart from breaking,
> I shall not live in vain;
> If I can ease one life the aching,
> Or cool one pain,
> Or help one lonely person
> Into happiness again
> I shall not live in vain.

Thank you Emily Dickinson for stating my mission so eloquently.

The mission of this book is to help you:

√ Enrich your life by guiding you toward discovering and articulating your needs, wants, aspirations, and desires.

√ Embrace a spiritual belief system that fosters the self-evident principles of integrity, trust, truth, love, patience, and growth as you strive to become your highest self.

√ Live life with discipline, courage, purpose, and a "spirit of adventure" while creating a plan to leave your greatest legacy—the gift of your true self.

CHAPTER ONE

A MIND/BODY/SPIRIT
CONNECTION
CAN SHAPE YOUR WORLD

"A human being is part of the whole, called by us "Universe"...The delusion (or separation) is a kind of prison for us...Our task must be to free ourselves from this prison by widening our circle of compassion to embrace all living creatures and the whole nature of its beauty." –Albert Einstein

For many people, the term "spirit" or "spirituality" has several different connotations. Some people define spirituality in a strictly religious fashion, while others relate it as an "essence" of either goodness or evil. For the purpose of this book, let's define spirituality as a "call to authenticity and wholeness." In this case, it is an undeniable force that lies within each of us, yet beyond us. It drives and inspires us to seek greater meaning as we experience life.

As we allow our spirituality to continually guide and support new directions, we discover a new meaning and philosophy of life that supports symbolic unity. This driving force inspires and guides us toward continually questioning, seeking, and discovering renewal and growth. At the same time, our spirit extends an invitation to reform and transform so we can achieve a deepened connection with God.

Since spirituality represents the core of our authentic self, it is no wonder that it magnifies the pure God-like nature that emanates from us and resonates with love. Our spirituality fosters a language and understanding that serves to open up our hearts and minds to become more of who we truly are and less of who we have become conditioned to be.

THE CONNECTION BETWEEN SPIRITUALITY AND GOD

The parochial definition of "God" does not adequately cover the scope of God's existence or greatness. I define God as the ever-loving spirit that exists and moves within and outside of us. God's spirit is beyond the physical or sensorial world we know. God can be intuition or the silence we go to for listening.

Spirituality is the relationship and experience of God as a process. As we create our lives in relationship with God, each other, and ourselves, we are able to experience how God relates to us and how we respond. Striving for greater meaning and purpose in our lives requires us to question our beliefs, evaluate them, and make choices that enable us to create spiritual beliefs based in truth and love. It is these very truths that become the purpose of our spiritual life.

The dynamic and pervasive force we experience is the Universal Spirit of God that continually changes and matures us. Spirituality invites those of us who believe to a process of transformation. Becoming unconditioned to the ways of the world and becoming aligned with our highest truths and nature enables us as believers to understand how to heighten our humanity. This developmental and evolutionary growth enhances our awareness and appreciation of faith, trust, gratitude, acceptance, compassion, service, and joy.

As we grow in spirit and deepen our relationship with God, we learn to embody our mind, body, and spirit toward an enlightening and empowering force that is present in all living things. We begin to learn how our needs can be spiritually fulfilled. This is what connects our humanity with divinity. We discover that the path to God and spirituality is one of self-awareness.

QUESTIONING YOUR WAY TO CONSCIOUS LIVING

Part of enhancing our spirituality is the continuing quest to learn to live in the present in a conscious, mindful way. In fact, when many people begin their spiritual journey, they find it to be a healing process in which their focus and concentration is on the question: "How does one live consciously?"

16

With the advent of the millennium, we may very well have experienced another type of "Copernican Revolution" as it relates to our Models of Reality. Copernicus' Theory turned the physical universe inside out by putting the Sun, not the Earth, at the center of the Universe. A similar experience is occurring with our current models of reality, where they need to be turned inside out by placing consciousness firmly at the center. It is a process that requires us to go beyond our objective realities, which constitute approximately 97% of who we are and what we project in any given situation.

During the course of your spiritual journey, you will realize the necessity, importance, and meaning of "going into the desert" to question, search, reconcile, and integrate life's most valuable experiences. It will be a vital process of your own self-discovery that focuses on uncovering your truest essence, which will help you live consciously on all levels.

You will also develop various philosophical points of view that will eventually pave the way for a liberating belief system. It will become apparent that life is not black or white; it is about living in the gray area, in ambiguity. Although we consider ourselves creatures of habit, we are part of a process that is continually evolving in which change is the only constant. Metaphorically put, it is as though we are like two musical notes that are always in discord.

Discover Your Spiritual Essence

Our culture belongs to a strategic mindset that wants safety. The human tragedy exists in our belief that we must choose between the world we perceive as safe and the world of the unknown. In actuality, we belong solely to neither. As a result of our confusion, we have become conditioned and entrained. It has become increasingly difficult to identify our individuality within the confines of our tribes or collective mind groups, since they operate with rules that produce fear, sacrifice, and conformity. The challenge is to define our own spiritual essence and individuality and find ways in which to maintain that identity

within the confines of a particular group. Sometimes it is doable and other times it is not.

To elaborate my point, let's consider some of the social and economic issues involved with life in these confusing times. Today more than ever we are dealing with issues of time poverty. We feel as if there is never enough time to do all the things we want to do. This makes it increasingly more important for us to develop our lives without being totally selfish. The dichotomy of this situation may provoke the question "Why?" Why do we feel we have no time? Perhaps the answer lies in our belief patterns that prompt us to have certain expectations and that lend themselves toward the creation of our attitudes. Because we believe we have no time, it becomes true. However, if we believe we do have the time we need to accomplish our goals, then that, too, becomes true. Our attitude and our beliefs becomes the map of how we perceive the world. Remember what Buddha said, "Reality is not what you see; it is what you don't see."

The strength of the human spirit lies in its incredible diversity. There is always an opportunity and a place for us to see the world though the eyes of others and grow. Discovering our spiritual essence is about listening, understanding, respecting, confronting, and transforming. The strength of America and its people has always and will continue to lie within its diversity. By embracing this diversity and having full belief in ourselves, we can begin to discover the true essence of our being.

THE POWER TO CREATE THE LIFE OF YOUR DREAMS

Have you ever thought of your life as a work of art? Metaphorically, perhaps you may want to think about it as a piece of clay. As you, the artist, sculpt a piece of clay, it takes on several different forms during the process. Often, the end result is not what we expected.

As we journey through life, we sculpt our lives, and the process is rather ambiguous. Issues that create stress become increasingly apparent. We resist rather than surrender, and we become attached to certain outcomes rather than just "go with the flow," learn from the experience, and let go of expectations. This implies that the problem is not always in the belief itself, but in our attachment to it. The price of attachment is often a sacrifice of objectivity. The necessity to switch from belief to faith is a provocative thought—one that is clearly a necessity as we traverse through unchartered waters.

Often times I have been known to say: "Happiness is not always what we want; it is often what we get." This does not mean that we do not experience the discomfort or pain of various situations that unfold, such as the loss of a business deal or even a job. It means there is a reason for the madness around us, and I believe it is because the Spirit has better things in store for us.

This does not negate the feeling that often times it is humanly difficult for us to readily accept change without having been prepared. The idea, however, is to savor life and be grateful for those growthful moments of both despair and joy. Be mindful that this is life, and it is filled with many surprises as we journey along our paths.

HARNESS THE BEAUTY OF YOUR INDIVIDUALITY IN ORDER TO CONTRIBUTE TO THE WHOLE

There is no doubt that we possess the knowledge and the inner resources to grow individually and collectively. Our individuality and uniqueness manifest in countless ways. There are no two people who think, feel, or speak the same way. Each of us is unique and special. Our gifts are uniquely ours, and it is for us to decide how we want to nurture and develop these gifts. There is a wellspring of genius and passion ready to soar inside each and every one of us. This is our soul, our voice. It cries out for freedom for us to be who we want to be and who we can be. Therefore, the work of the soul is to wake up the self, and its foundation is one of self-knowledge and acceptance.

As we artfully live out our lives, our hearts and minds continually seek a new balance of growth and harmony. When we achieve this, we are able to live and persevere in a life of

change without the fear of "not knowing." It is this experience that preserves and feeds the soul. We go to ourselves, learn to know and understand ourselves, and find ways to fulfill ourselves. The more fulfilled we become, the closer we approach our authentic self.

As a society at large, we have been undergoing the transition from an old paradigm of parent/child, whereby people were told what to do and how to do it, to a new paradigm of adult, which emphasizes people taking charge or ownership. Let me illustrate this point by using corporations as a metaphor. Interestingly enough, the same issues that exist in a corporation or business entity are the same ones that exist within the individuals, namely the need to create a mission and vision, devise goals, values, beliefs, and define behaviors.

In view of the prevailing economic and social changes, companies are under pressure to be more competitive, productive, and cost efficient so they can survive in a continually changing economic climate. Employees are feeling the effects of these changes and finding themselves in positions of responsibility without the necessary skills to do their job. There are challenges and constraints that face management as well, such as dealing with massive change and restructured organizations with fewer people to do the work. And throughout it all, everyone, from senior management to the entry-level employee, is experiencing increasing demands. To keep up, it is not enough to simply reinvent corporations. It is now understood that the mind, spirit, involvement, creativity, and passion of the worker are every bit as important as the external machination of the management.

The need now exists to create an environment that fosters a sense of cooperation, commitment, trust, and respect, where people and businesses can align their mission, vision, and goals toward mutual creativity, productivity, community, and esprit de corps. When both parties are meeting needs, wants, aspirations, and values, this place is possible. If businesses want people to be creative and adaptive, then it behooves them to invest in their people. When they do so, they are also investing in themselves.

Communication and relationship building are vital to team building as well, whereby each individual can add his or her value. When Gandhi was giving advice to leaders, he said, "You must become the change you want to see in the world." And before Gandhi there was Socrates who said, "Let him who would move the world, first move himself." This kind of growth and development is first necessary on an intrapersonal level. Then it expands to an interpersonal level. We project who we are in our relationships, and the issues we dislike or like in others are often a reflection of our own internal issues. It is crucial to integrate all the parts of us from a mental, physical, and spiritual perspective. Then the joy, peace, harmony, balance, and fulfillment create an internal synergy that is congruent with our own true nature. As we view our work from the inside out, we will discover a new commonality where we can trust and support each other along the way.

Discovering and empowering the self creates a definitive sense of purpose. In your life this is an integral part of your nature and being. As you engage in the process of transformation, you begin to identify your uniqueness and passion, resulting in growth, achievement, and a better world. Once you decide to enrich your life and discover what it is you need, want, and desire, you can create a personal mission statement as to who you are.

The Foundation of Your Spirituality

There is no mistake that we are all on purpose. Our existence is a Divine Gift, and our mission gives us a purpose and sense of direction to go forward. When you begin working on a mission statement and experiencing the process of literally defining it, the extraordinary sense of who you are, what you want to do, and where you want to go begins taking various shapes and directions.

This foundation becomes the cornerstone for you to set goals, boundaries, establish new beliefs, and continually evaluate the process. Some of the questions to ask are "What does this mean?" "What is it I need to do?" "What are the resources

I have that will enable me to accomplish what I want to do?" and "How do I go about accomplishing this goal or task?" This is a partial view of what recreating the self is about.

These experiences are different for everyone. The answers and non-answers to many of our life questions enable us to realize and understand the workings of the "Universe," Spirit, God, or whatever you choose to call this magnificent Presence that surrounds, protects, watches over, and loves us. This supportive guardianship heightens our sense of growth and knowledge as it attracts us to serendipitous friendships and working relationships with other like-minded individuals.

The Spirit works in many ways and opens up several doors. When we consciously live in the present and focus our energies in that place, synchronicity unfolds and serendipitous happenings occur at such a rapid pace. Unfortunately, sometimes when our plates are too full or if we find ourselves preoccupied, we often miss the message.

A few years ago I read a brief story regarding the value of "your message." As Mahatma Gandhi boarded a train in India, a reporter asked him if he had a message for the people. Ironically, it was Gandhi's day of silence, so he scribbled a note that read, "My life is my message." When you understand that everything about you tells something about what is in you, you pay more attention and live your life with greater intention. As we start to live consciously and mindfully, we are able to listen and receive. This listening can be as involved as hearing the words of a song or the chance utterance of another's words, or it can be as simple as listening to the whisper of the birds, trees, rivers, oceans, or just plain silence. For all of this we experience a sense of gratitude that creates a well of emotion that cannot be described or explained, only felt.

EMBRACE THE JOYS AND SORROWS THAT CREATE YOUR LIFE'S MISSION

The bottom line is that we are all here on purpose with a specific mission, and the process of understanding, growing, and developing ourselves is refined through our own experiences.

As we engage in the "refinement process" we become more of our magnificent selves; we learn to manage and use our gifts of Grace from God to endure, reconcile, forgive, love, and heal others and ourselves. Just as the experiences we encounter refine us, so too do we refine the experience in such a way as to give it back. Before we can empower others, we need to learn how to first empower ourselves. It is this sense of self-empowerment that is a necessary ingredient for us to meet the challenges associated with our life purpose and mission. This is the manner in which God or the Goddess shares His or Her completeness with us.

Always remember that we all possess various talents and gifts, and as we use our unique abilities, they illuminate a feeling of magic within us. As we channel expressions of love, whether they be through prayer or work, we establish deep connections that make the rite of passage safe. Just as the Magis' gifts to the Christ child were sold to bring safe passage to Jesus, the same is true for all of us as we channel God's love and embrace our spirituality. In essence "We are bringing our gifts for the safe passage of others." It all fits into place.

The gift of the following chapters is to empower you to go on your journey of self-discovery with the assurance of having a "safe place" while being guided through the process of exploration, experience, awakening, and growth. This process of opening your heart while being encouraged to reach yourself through expressions of art and listening occur simultaneously. Every human being is creative and can on any level express him or herself artistically through painting, drawing, sculpting, craftsmanship, or writing.

Our lives are filled with endless stories. They represent the joys and sorrows that enable us to create our lives as a masterpiece, knowing that in the end our perpetual and eternal work of art is exactly the way it was meant to be.

CHAPTER TWO

CREATE A
STRONG & SUCCESSFUL
PERSONAL FOUNDATION

"Even though you may want to move forward in your life, you may have one foot on the brakes. In order to be free, we must learn how to let go. Release the hurt. Release the fear. Refuse to entertain your old pain. The energy it takes to hang onto the past is holding you back from a new life. What is it you would let go of today?" –Mary Manin Morrissey, author

As you embark on your journey to personal and spiritual growth, the first step is to deal with issues of the past and come to closure. Therapy, coupled with self-help books and support groups, are a powerful force in freeing yourself from past limitations. By examining your past you can learn how to live in the present and how to plan toward the future.

The purpose of this self-reflection is to develop a conscious "personal foundation" that will support your "new self" – a congruent self that is true to you. It means going through the purification ritual and getting rid of everything that holds you back. In essence, you are shifting from an old self that has been conditioned with learned patterns to a new self that is centered in truth and love instead of fear.

Think about life as a twofold process. The first part involves personality formation. We are born with pure sensation and spontaneity, and we learn through pain, pleasure, and imitation. We then develop a self-image of who we are, a self-ideal of how we want to be, and a self-esteem that varies and stays high without effort only when we attain a healthy level of self-worth. It is the root of our belief systems.

In some ways there is a dichotomy that exists here. For the most part, individuals tend to be creatures of habit, yet we

are continually evolving. This in and of itself represents an inner incongruity, because these images constitute a self-concept that originates with our belief patterns. We end up believing one of two scenarios – either "I'm OK" or "I'm not OK." These beliefs prompt us to have expectations that lend themselves toward the creation of our attitudes.

As we change, we sometimes get stuck because of belief patterns that get in the way and limit our potential. To observe this for yourself, find a partner and describe a situation that you would like to change. Observe your attitude and define it, and then think about your expectations and verbalize what they specifically are. Finally, hook into this state and define what your limiting belief is.

Before we get to the stage of questioning ourselves with regard to our beliefs and determining whether or not they are helpful or harmful to us, let's delve deeper and reflect on the questions in the following exercise. These questions will enable you to expand the exploration of your beliefs so you can achieve insights about yourself while effectively restructuring your personal reality.

QUESTIONS TO PONDER:
- *What are my beliefs about spirituality, my relationships, money, government, work, ability, health, family, future, and myself?*
- *Which beliefs work for or against me?*
- *Which beliefs do I want to keep and which ones do I want to add to the museum of old beliefs?*
- *What are the issues that stop me from doing what I want to do?*
- *What are my thoughts and feelings about change?*
- *How would I describe myself?*
- *What areas of my life do I want to work on?*

EXERCISE:

1. List three things you believe about yourself in each of the following categories: your relationships, money, government, work, ability, health, family, and future.
2. After each belief, note whether you experience the belief as either **Helpful**, by placing an "**H**" next to it, or as an **Obstacle**, by placing an "**O**" beside it.
3. After each belief, note whether you assumed the belief **Deliberately**, or whether you **Learned** it. Again, note it accordingly with a "**D**" or "**L**."

While you go through the above process be mindful of the following questions:
1. Does this belief support who I am or who I want to be?
2. Does this belief create a positive growth experience?
3. Does this belief improve my attitude?
4. Does this belief make me feel good or give me strength?
5. Does this belief align with my values and goals?

After you answer the above questions, evaluate your answers and determine why this particular belief makes you feel the way you do. During this process, allow yourself the space to get to know and understand yourself better, and at the same time enhance your intuitive side as you carefully listen to the words and the silence. Albert Einstein understood this concept rather well when he stated, "Few is the number of those who think with their own minds and feel with their own hearts."

The next step is to create a new empowering belief and ask yourself the same questions as above. Visualize how your new belief enables you to tap into your potential. Think about the pneumonic KASH, meaning do you have the *knowledge, attitude, skills,* and *habits* to support the new belief? If not, determine what actions you need to take to develop your KASH.

SUPPORTING YOUR OBJECTIVES
As you progress, remember the following principles: perseverance means courage, repetition is the mother of skill, and tenac-

ity is a sign of persistence. These are compelling ingredients that will move you toward your objectives.

When you create a new belief, metaphorically think of it as a table with legs. The belief is the tabletop, and the legs represent your ability to support the belief. For example, a teacher or parent may state the following new belief: "I am an asset who adds value to myself and others." Now, let's support that table belief with the following legs:

- I am worthy, capable, important, and have value to add.
- My value lies in the true essence of who I am.
- I am an effective listener who understands my students or children's needs, and I carefully pace and lead them toward a heightened sense of awareness and action.
- I have skill sets that enable my students or children to create the life and balance they desire.
- I continually seek new ways of learning and knowing, and I open myself to all possibilities of change and know that what happens is for the highest good of all.

When we think about our present state and then think about the desired state we want to achieve, we sometimes must address the elements that lie between points A and B. As you think about tasks you want to accomplish, you will discover various elements, such as *People, Behaviors,* and *Outcomes*. At this point, the questions to ask yourself are:

1. How *desirable* is the outcome?
2. What is the *possibility* of this outcome? Is there a motivational constraint?
3. Do I have the behavioral *capabilities* necessary to achieve this outcome?
4. Besides myself, who are the other people involved in achieving this outcome, and are we all *deserving and responsible*? Most important, am I deserving and responsible?
5. Are the people, behaviors, and outcome *clear and appropriate* for me?

After going through this belief self-assessment exercise you will have an idea where the gap or weak link exists. Once defined, you can proceed to determine where the motivation is lacking or needs shoring up.

THE EVOLUTIONARY PROCESS BEGINS

The next step focuses on being born to a new self. This is about the journey itself. Here is where we go into the desert and question, search, reconcile, and integrate our new learnings into our new beliefs. What evolves is the awareness and recognition of our true essence. As we de-program ourselves of who we were conditioned to be, the masks dissolve, and we no longer wear the facades of other hosts in our lives. Rather, we wear the true mask of who we are. We enter the place of light, love, peace, and joy.

There is no greater transformation than to experience the self-discovery of your unique, beautiful self. You are your greatest asset with unlimited potential who is worthy, capable, and important. Consider yourself the "Chosen One," a Divine Choice with a purpose. You are a Gift. The greatest travesty anyone could commit would be to not honor this special gift of themselves and to undermine their worth by comparing themselves to others.

When we don't recognize our gift to the world, we become discontent and irritable. Such was the case with "Bill," an entrepreneur who was dealing with the frustration of feeling bored in an industry that was no longer stimulating to him. By all accounts, Bill was a well-dressed, well-versed, confident, self-assured man with a high intellect and was a delight to be around. He had a confident presence about him, yet there was a part of him that was yearning to be creative. As we worked together, I discovered that in the past he performed in the theater. At the mention of this he would "light up."

To determine the source of Bill's discontentment, I asked him how he got into his present industry. He related the following story: When Bill was a senior in high school, his mother asked him what he wanted to do when he went to college. He

replied by saying he didn't know. His mother then asked him what he enjoyed doing, and he responded that he liked chemistry. Well, the decision was made. He was going to study chemical engineering, and he did.

Upon graduation Bill worked for a chemical distribution company. Years later he started his own enterprise and is quite successful to this day. Based on our conversation, I felt that he was satisfying the mental aspect of himself. He was truly talking and working from his mind; however, his heart was discontent. Something was missing, and that missing element was the ability to express his creativity in a complete sense.

I asked Bill what specifically he could do in his business that would tap into his creative resources. For example, could he create multimedia productions for his industry about the available services? After some deliberation, Bill's answer was positive. He believed he could create programs using multimedia presentations that were focused on upgrading the industry standards for clients, distributors, and manufacturers. It was a win-win relationship. This approach satisfied his creative side, and it also served a greater purpose within his industry.

As a result of this change, several things began to unfold. First, the Association recognized Bill's value and saw potential in this alliance that would benefit Bill, themselves, and the population they served. They appointed him a Board of Director's seat and asked him to take responsibility for the industry's education responsibilities. Because he was now in the public's eye, he began receiving invitations to be a keynote speaker. Bill eventually realized the potential to diversify his business by providing consulting services. This new direction enabled him to think along the lines of appointing a general manager to spearhead the chemical side of the business while he continued to do the things he loved. While Bill was successful in his business before, aligning himself with "who he is" equated an even higher level of inner peace, which ultimately relates to success. It is this integration of heart and mind that creates an inner congruity and sends out a congruous message to others.

THE BUSINESS OF YOU

To be good in business, the business needs to be about you. When we do what we love day after day and year after year, we eventually become what we love. It is no different than knowing and owning your name. Just as you know your name, it is equally important to know what you love. This is what opens up your heart, excites your spirit, and lives in your eyes. When you are mindful of what you love, that love will light up your life and ignite your passion. Then, when your passion kicks into gear, you want to work hard, you feel gratified, motivated, seek challenge, and suddenly your creativity and innovation are in full gear. You gain courage to embark on new journeys, you discover a sense of clarity of purpose, and the capacity to take action on what you believe falls into place comfortably.

Answer this question: "What percentage of the life you are living is actually yours?"

If you're like most people, the percentage is quite small. Throughout our lives, parents, teachers, friends, and family teach us their beliefs and views. We blindly accept many of these teachings as absolute truth, and we carry them with us through life. However, when we take the time to question the beliefs we hold, we give ourselves the opportunity to truly own the beliefs as ours.

For example, think about the number of adults who return to college. Many of these people have experienced professors whose thinking is diametrically opposed to their ideology (the views they had been conditioned to). Many of these adults say that these experiences were painful, when in reality, some of these teachers proved to be quite extraordinary. The pain of shaking their foundation coupled with the high levels of anxiety was the down side. The up side was the growthful experience of challenging their long-held views. When these adults became open to questioning, they were able to assess their true beliefs and discard the ones that were not congruent with their values. As a result of this experience, these people emotionally grew and learned different ways of experiencing others and them-

selves. Evaluating different maps of the world always proves to be an extraordinarily growthful experience.

WHAT ARE YOUR BELIEFS?

When you analyze your past, you can begin to find new choices where none seemed to exist; develop a sense of self responsibility and balance in relation to others; achieve a compelling sense of personal fulfillment; reap gifts of knowledge, commitment, harmony, and joy; and learn to love, laugh, and give. To do this effectively, take a good look at your beliefs. Are they positive or negative, energizing or draining? Do they promote or block your achievements? What would happen if you believed that you have the power to do the things you want to do and be the kind of person you want to be? Stop and think about that statement because it is quite powerful.

When we talk about beliefs, we are really talking about how we each see our world. We form beliefs as a result of hearing, seeing, and observing an event. As we process the event, we form a specific idea, which may be negative or positive, and over time multiple experiences create a cluster of beliefs. For example, a friend of mine has an incredible fear of dogs. When he was a child he heard a dog barking. Before he knew it, the dog was chasing him. His initial belief of dogs became: "I don't like dogs because they are noisy, mean, and chase people." After multiple experiences of seeing, hearing, and interacting with different types of dogs who were both friendly and not so friendly, his negative belief evolved into a group of possible beliefs that were more specific in nature. For example, "German Sherpards are mean, Dachshunds are sweet and loving, and Bull Mastivs are slobbery and drool too much." These clusters of beliefs, whether negative or positive, clearly generate emotions and feelings about what something means. It is this evolutionary process that becomes our hierarchy of attitudes, values, and worldview.

YOUR VIEWPOINT AND BELIEF SYSTEM

In 1928, Eduard Spranger, a German psychologist, teacher and philosopher, wrote a book entitled *Types of Men*. The book detailed six types of people each with a specific arena of activity, attitudes, and values. The value identities we will discuss are the by-product of work done by Eduard Spranger (1882-1962), Gordon Willard Allport (1897-1967), and most recent Bill J. Bonnstetter of Target Training International, Ltd. The six attitude types are Theoretical, Utilitarian, Aesthetic, Social, Individualistic, and Traditional.

Each person has a viewpoint in each of the six attitudes, although two are most dominant. The top two attitudes in the hierarchy serve to impel a person to act in a way that will fulfill a particular value. Because attitudes tend to interact with one another, this action influences the other four attitudes. From these attitudes we form a sense of purpose and direction to our lives from which we positively value or negatively judge people, places, things, and experiences. Our model of the world becomes a filter through which we think and look at life. It is this model that supports our view of who we are and what values we hold dear. Our values are the "Why we do the things we do," which stimulate and drive our behaviors. Later we will identify these values, observe ways in which they might interact with one another, and find the keys to unlock the doors to our own passion.

Eighty percent of our behaviors are needs driven, thereby creating wants that serve to motivate us. When those wants are fulfilled, your needs are met and your values are satisfied. The underlying principle is that motivation occurs from a combination of two driving forces: pain and pleasure (also known as reward). Metaphorically speaking, you could use a tack on a chair to represent pain and a circle with a reward in it to represent pleasure. To accomplish anything, we need both pain and pleasure to drive us toward action and move us from one environment to another. This action occurs because of one of three things: 1) we self-inflict it, 2) others inflict it, or 3) the environment inflicts it. To master all these elements, create a scenario

of accountability for each: be accountable to yourself, to someone else, and to the environment in which you work or live.

The reasoning behind this is simple: Often times when people lack motivation, it's a result of their unwillingness to put the tack on the chair and to be accountable to someone to do tough things. For example, there are those of us who may want to lose a few pounds. If we want to lose weight, we can offer to pay someone to hold us accountable to lose the weight. Perhaps this is enough motivation for some people. On the other hand, perhaps we want to wager a bet with someone that we will lose the weight, and if we fail, we will pay them. This second scenario makes someone so accountable to themselves that they will lose the weight because they don't want to pay another their hard-earned money.

Because your values define who you are, you will cry out to get them fulfilled. Therefore, it is vital to identify your attitudes and values, because your two top attitudes will drive your actions. If your career and activities are in line with this passion, you will find fulfillment in life. If they are not, you will be unable to achieve your fullest potential in an environment that is not indigenous to who you are. Think of it like a plant. A cactus from Arizona will never grow and flourish in Colorado no matter how much water and fertilizer you give it. In terms of yourself, consider the following questions:

- Have you ever been in a job that just didn't seem to fit or feel right?
- Have you ever experienced a level of motivation that slowly diminished from the start?
- What happened to your self-esteem in the process of either of those events?

If your self-esteem suffered, then it is likely that a negative belief such as "I can't do it" began to appear on the horizon. Then, the self-perpetuating cycle of failure and sabotage showed their true colors as you went through the agony of losing the desire to try, experiencing diminished success and recognition, exerting less effort and perseverance, and finally cul-minating in "zeroing" yourself out.

Herein lies the connection between values and behav-iors. Up to now, our values tell us "Why we do the things we do" whether they are driven by pain, pleasure, or both and whether they are inflicted by self, other, or the environment. Then once we move from point A to point B we are responding with the "How we do things" part of ourselves. It is the method-ology of how we act, and depending upon our behavioral style we may choose to feel angry, distrustful, emotional, or fearful followed by a response to fight, flee, or submit. Often submis-sion creates physical illness, because when we feel stuck, the mind goes on overload. When this occurs, these symptoms un-consciously begin to take a toll on our body's cellular structure, resulting in "Dis-Ease," meaning unpleasant feelings or loss of pleasure. The key is to discover your passion and find the right environment for your unique self so you can flourish.

Gandhi said it best in this way:

Keep your thoughts positive;
Thoughts become your words.
Keep your words positive;
Words become your behaviors.
Keep your behaviors positive;
Behaviors become your habits.
Keep your habits positive;
Habits become your values.
Keep your values positive;
Values become your destiny.

You are your thoughts. You can be whatever you want to be. There is a deep tendency in human nature to become precisely like that which you habitually imagine yourself to be. When Anwar el Saddat wrote his book, *In Search of Identity*, he included a great quote: "He who could not change the very fabric of his thought will never be able to change reality." Tho-mas Edison put it succinctly when we said, "Restlessness is discontent and discontent is the first necessity."

THE POWER OF CHANGE

As you embark on your spiritual journey, you will experience a mindful workout. You will form a partnership with yourself during this time of change while having the assurance of the book that there is support as you develop your inner strength. This is vital during a time of change, since we are dealing with external and internal factors. External refers to the environment, which we have little or no control of; and internal means the transition and ambiguity you feel within yourself. You will experience a sense of evolution and revolution going on at the same time, which is a prerequisite for being able to anticipate change and take steps to meet it. Evolutionary change is more or less orderly, whereas revolutionary change is chaotic. Because the change you feel will be more revolutionary than evolutionary, the change is not orderly and you cannot avoid its impact. So if you wait, you miss the opportunity to experience and grow.

As Frederick Nietzsche explained: "One must have chaos in one's self in order to give birth to a dancing star."

Change is a way the Universe brings us closer to the truth. Getting coached through the process is about dealing with the internal changes first and then developing a plan of action. The clarity, structure of a plan, and support of a coaching resource will give sustainability to a given situation. When you can sustain new ways of being, you can begin to accept the idea's greatness and envision its limitless potential. You can then create an enriching life that is joyful, adventurous, and fun.

When making a change, ask yourself the following questions to determine what is it you are truly thinking and feeling:
1. Why do I want to make a change?
2. At which one of the following stages do I see myself in relationship to making the change?
   - √ Pre-Contemplation: Not thinking of Change
   - √ Contemplation: Seriously Thinking of Change
   - √ Preparation: Getting Ready to Make a Change
   - √ Action: Actively Making the Change

√   Maintenance: Made the Change and Maintaining Change for Greater than Six Months

3. What am I willing to do to make the change?
4. What specifically do I need to do to make the change?
5. What are the pros and cons to making the change?
6. What other options should I consider in relation to making this change?
7. How do I feel about this change (before and after)? Is it alignment with who I am, what I want to be, do, and have?
8. What are the possible solutions and which seems the best?
9. Am I willing to take this risk?
10. What specifically is holding me back?
11. What are the actions I need to take?
12. How will I take these actions?
13. When will I start?

   This sort of questioning forces you to identify and dismantle belief systems that stand in the way of you achieving your potential. Understand that for change to be successful, first there is a feeling of discontent and tension. This, coupled with the dissatisfaction and desire to want to change, plus having a plan of action, equates success.

DISSATISFACTION x PLAN x ACTION = SUCCESSFUL CHANGE
For example, if the dissatisfaction is equal to 50, and the plan is equal to 0, then nothing will happen: $50 \times 0 = 0$. If any component is equal to zero, then there is no progress toward the desired change. Obviously, the higher the variables, the greater the probability for success. This type of change is "inspirational," meaning it comes from within. When change is inspirational, people have been known to soar beyond their highest expectations as they incur lasting change. On the other hand, when people want to change as a result of fear, then the change usually doesn't have a lasting effect. A typical example would be a heart patient who is frightened of dying, loses weight, and then is not able to maintain the weight loss and goes back to his or her old habits.

Once you understand these concepts, then the other ingredients of this "success process" are a positive belief, a positive attitude, and a strong commitment. When you combine all these factors, you are unstoppable. You can jump into any situation with both feet and create magical results.

EXERCISE:

Determine what's most important to you in your life and what is it that gives your life meaning. In addition, ask yourself the following questions and think about some of the ways this coaching process may be instrumental to you in your own progress.

1. Describe yourself behaviorally.
2. Where are you most irresponsible in your life?
3. Who is in charge of your life – you or other people?
4. What boundaries do you have in place?
5. What are your needs and wants?
6. What are the three important things you would like to accomplish in your life now?
7. What price would you place on achieving them?
8. What is the biggest business or personal opportunity you are currently not taking advantage of?
9. What activity do you get involved with that puts a smile on your face?
10. What is your special talent you would like to orient your life around?
11. Where do you get your energy from – yourself or others?
12. Where are you putting your energy – in the past, present, or future?

Take all the time you need to respond to the above questions. Clearly, it is an opportunity to take an introspective view of yourself and get to the heart of what is going on in your life. By doing this, you can discover how important it is to follow the Socratic proverb, which emphasizes the notion that before we can know the world around us and make wise choices, we first need to "Know Thyself."

CHAPTER THREE

CREATE A
MISSION WITH
A VISION

"Your work is to discover your work, and then with all your heart to give yourself to it." –Buddha

With your strong personal foundation in place, the next step is to create a mission. Your personal mission is vital because it gives you clarity, which is important for knowing, understanding, and growing yourself. Your mission is a specific, one-sentence description of what you are committed to in your life, and it consists of three main elements:

1. A statement that is easily communicated to someone else.
2. A statement that is powerful enough to move you where you want to go.
3. A statement that is clear enough to allow you to recognize your accomplishment after you have achieved your goal.

YOU ARE YOUR MISSION

Creating a mission statement is a necessity primarily because it is what we are all about. It is our sense of purpose, which is an integral part of our nature. Think about it this way: When you develop a true sense of *who you are*, you no longer have to be *who you are not*. Isn't this what success is all about, not what you do but who you are and how you align your work with your uniqueness?

When your mission is clear, you can make the transition from an inner life focus of being to an outer life focus of doing. It is up to each of us to take responsibility and to unite these two parts of ourselves while putting our spirits to work. So a

mission is essentially a manifestation of our individuality that is larger than our role in life. It requires a big picture orientation that needs to be in alignment with our core values. Carl Jung succinctly stated the message when he declared, "Your vision will become clear only when you look into your heart. Who looks outside, dreams; who looks inside, awakens."

Your essence, your sense of purpose, and your identity come from your heart. Pay close attention to the things that are closest to your heart and cling to them as you would your life, because without them, life can be meaningless. This is your truth and your gift to yourself and others. Truth comes from your heart, and accuracy comes from your mind. While the heart has the answers, the mind has the questions. That's why it is important to keep a balance because they both have positive intentions and can be highly effective when they work in tandem with one another.

As we contemplate the complexities of the mind and heart, let us be aware that the word "heart" is composed of three words: "Art" as we "Hear" with our "Ear." We each have the amazing ability to translate the language of the heart with the "Art of Listening." When you hear with your ear, how many times do you hear yet not listen? However, when you listen with your heart, your creative juices start flowing and allow for some artful expression, whether it be literary, artistic, or some other form. *The Little Prince* states, "It is only with the heart that one can see rightly…What is essential is invisible." Couple this knowingness with a belief that your personal and business life is about you. When this happens you have found your "treasure," because wherein your heart lies so lies your treasure.

The discovery of your passion enables you to want to work and play hard, reaping a sense of gratification and motivation that seeks challenge and triggers more creativity and innovation. When Gandhi spoke of passion and service, there was an air of spiritual elegance and truth to his statement, "Service which is rendered without joy helps neither the servant nor the served."

DISCOVERING THE PURPOSE OF YOUR MISSION

As we seek greater meaning in life, we often make desperate attempts toward seeking a professional life with a purposeful mission. Such was the case with "Bob," a man who had extraordinary gifts, talents, and abilities, yet who went from one frustrating situation to another. Throughout it all, Bob knew he was capable of great things, yet he had an unexplainable feeling of unhappiness.

Although Bob could do many things and generally succeeded at various jobs; the continual pressure of having to push so hard to achieve and accomplish suddenly took a toll in the form of severe burnout and depression. All the money, highflying deals, and material possessions contributed toward the maintenance of a lifestyle that sustained and supported a quick fix. For Bob, more was never enough. Ultimately, his possessions started to own him, causing emptiness and despair to settle in.

Unable to handle his self-created prison, Bob began asking himself questions, such as "Who am I?" "What do I want to do with my life?" and "What kind of career do I want for myself?" Deep down, Bob wanted to "feel' once again, and he did not want to live his life as though on auto pilot. Ultimately, the question became "What is my life's mission and purpose?"

Rather than spend his life "doing," Bob wanted to discover his "being" and then go and "do" what it was that gave him joy, peace, contentment, and fulfillment. After a number of coaching sessions Bob was able to identify the missing ingredients in his personal and professional life and apply his renewed sense of joy and compassion. During this process Bob identified several activities that were gratifying. He eventually singled out the one evening a week when he taught a business course at a major university as the highlight of his life and the thing that gave him the most satisfaction.

Shortly thereafter Bob gave up his position as a corporate CEO and took a full time faculty position. Today, in spite of a significant decrease in salary, he approaches each workday with enthusiasm, creativity, and positive anticipation. The sat-

isfaction of sharing his knowledge and experience with business school students added a new and expanded dimension to his life.

QUESTIONS TO PONDER:
♦ ***What is my mission?***
♦ ***Am I happy in what I am doing or am I going from one miserable situation to another?***

EXERCISE:

Take the time now to create a personal mission statement, an expression of your individuality and uniqueness. To do so, ask yourself the following questions:

1. What do I want to accomplish?
2. How specifically can I accomplish it?
3. Why do I really want to do this?
4. What are some of the ways in which I will accomplish it?
5. What is involved with doing this?
6. What price am I willing to pay?

Reflect on your answers so you can fill in the blanks to the next statement. It answers the question: "Who are you?"

"I AM____THAT_____THE_____WITH_____."

Perhaps the following example of my personal mission statement will serve to guide you through the exercise. "I am a messenger that sends energy to connect truths for the client with love, understanding, passion, and a spirit of adventure."

Determine what it is you truly believe about yourself and how that belief can contribute to the greater good. By doing this, you can understand what Dostoyevky meant when he said, "For the secret of man's being is not only to live but to have something to live for." What do you want to live for?

CHAPTER FOUR

DEFINE, UNDERSTAND, AND EMPLOY ENERGY

"When you're following your energy and doing what you want all the time, the distinction between work and play dissolves."
–Shakti Gawain

All things have energy – people, animals, plants, buildings, and everything else on Earth. We are fields of energy and information, and it is this force that flows within us, through us, between us, and among us. Our energy is intelligent and constantly in motion.

The more evolved we become as human beings, the more efficiently we use our energy. For example, as we open up in our relationships with a parent, child or significant other and learn to accept them and love them for who they are without having a need to change them, there is a special love that feels blissful with no words that can adequately describe the feeling. Just as we have the potential to experience this deepened type of love for another, we also have the potential to feel the sadness that might accompany a possible loss. Bearing this in mind, be aware that the person with a high level of sensitivity is far more susceptible to utilizing energy to enrich or heal, harm or deplete themselves. Our wholeness in terms of harmony and well-being are at stake.

DISCOVER YOUR ENERGY SOURCE
We each derive our energy from many sources. First are the internal sources such as the values and beliefs that drive us and demonstrate "why" we do things. These internal triggers translate into our external behavioral forms.

Consider the following examples:

- Imagine a teacher tutoring a student who is struggling to understand algebraic concepts and principles. When the student finally "gets it" and new learnings come together, it is an inspirational moment for both teacher and student. Moments like these are energizing, symbolic, and represent an inspirational energy form. "Inspirational" means "in spirit," and when we are in spirit, we experience an extraordinary sense of joy, contentment, satisfaction, and fulfillment.

- Imagine an athlete who has always wanted to compete in the Olympics and win a gold medal for his or her country. The inner passion of this determined athlete drives him or her toward an action that is demanding, decisive, and challenging toward a productive, results-oriented goal.

- Imagine a mystic who uses the breath to relax, meditate, or energize him or herself. Depending upon how this person uses the breath determines the desired energy level. The breath as a life force can be utilized in slow, rhythmic cycles to enhance relaxation or meditation, or in quick, forceful cycles to ignite more energy.

These examples show how we each derive our energy from different sources. Some of us receive energy from the adrenaline rush of physical challenge, others from the unified screams and cheers for the home team to score another touchdown, and still others derive it from the beautiful verses of a poem. Whether it be standing before a Van Gogh, making a speech in front of hundreds of people, listening in solitude to LaBoheme, or being part of a closely-knit team, all people have a path to heightened energy.

Our values, beliefs, and behavioral styles have much to do with the things that serve to energize us. And so, these exemplify how each person derives his or her own energy within as well as outside themselves.

On the other hand, when we are not aligned with our values and beliefs, our personal and professional lives suffer. Motivation becomes lost, and the need to have to push rather than feeling the burning passionate desire of being pulled toward something becomes a struggle as well as a necessity. Consider the following examples:

- Imagine being in a job where you feel as though you are giving your all and not receiving enough. Perhaps this is an unappreciative environment where you do not feel seen or heard.

- Imagine feeling pushed to produce beyond your natural limit, causing you to feel exhausted and drained. Perhaps you need to set boundaries or evaluate whether the values of the company are so different from yours that it is absolutely the wrong environment for you.

- Imagine feeling a loss of interest in what you used to enjoy. Perhaps you have outgrown what you are doing and need a drastic change.

- Imagine over promising someone and not being able to keep your word. Perhaps this is part of an adrenaline addiction that temporarily serves to control you until such time when you "burn out." The question is "who is controlling who and where is the energy coming from?"

Disempowering situations such as these, coupled with the cups of coffee or candy bars we need to stimulate us enough to keep going, do nothing to preserve our energy and can certainly create havoc over time. Just as these points are worthy of consideration, so are the personal experiences we encounter when we feel disappointed for not having gotten ahead as quickly as expected.

In extreme cases when a person feels disconnected from his or her core feelings, the person's inclination is to seek artificial stimuli. These outlets serve to initially provide a quick start that temporarily sustains the person. However, that initial feeling quickly dissipates, leaving the person with a need for more until more is not enough. Dangerous and reckless behavior, confrontation, road rage, alcohol, and barbiturates are some of the desperate attempts that people make to feel better. Others may turn to compulsive shopping, gambling, coffee, or sugars, which represent other forms of external energy sources. All these options end up harming an individual when taken to extremes.

Based upon your own individual make up, take a few moments to reflect on your sources of personal energy and determine whether they are positive or negative. If they are positive, they will excite, energize, and drive you toward your potential. If they are negative, they will deplete and exhaust your reserves. The following questions to ponder will help you establish a clear sense of the forces and reserves within you.

QUESTIONS TO PONDER:

♦ *How much energy do I have and where do I draw it from?*

♦ *Does my energy come from a cup of coffee, a bottle of soda, or from my core?*

♦ *Do I get my energy from a problem-free environment or a crisis-oriented one that thrives on adrenaline?*

♦ *Where am I spending my energy? Where am I now? Am I in the present, past, or future? If I am putting my energy in the past, am I dead or alive? If the past is dead, and I am directing my energy in the past, then am I in a dead or alive space? The same holds true for the future. Is energy spent in the future dead because the future is not yet here?*

♦ *What are the tolerances in my life? What takes my energy that ordinarily would be directed toward meaningful and productive directions?*

♦ *Are these tolerances a result of not drawing boundaries against the abuses of others, or are they a result of a lack of willingness and language to communicate what behavior is acceptable or not acceptable?*

A REAL-LIFE ENERGY CRISIS

Inefficiently using your energy can have profound effects. When a group of people come together and inefficiently use their energy as a whole, the effects can be devastating. A corporate client of mine experienced this challenge first hand and as a result gained some valuable insights into the resources that were essential to their success.

The company was in the midst of some pressing problems, namely frustration and conflict among employees, low productivity, declining morale, and high turnover. When management decided to "reinvent" the organization in order to breathe new life into it, the problems only escalated, resulting in further chaos. The executives knew they needed to create an atmosphere of win-win relationships. The question was, "How?"

There were several directions this company needed to pursue, and one by one they did. During the process of restructuring, company leaders focused on their greatest asset, their people. Unfortunately, when a no-win situation exists, people will either fight, flee, or submit. These particular employees chose to fight, resulting in a high organizational stress level. People were leaving the company in record numbers, and those who were staying seemed to ration their efforts and pursued their own private agendas. To quickly alleviate some of these issues, we first provided the employees with a sense of support and reassurance. In addition, it was necessary for them to develop an awareness of what their job requirements were, what was expected of them, and how their behavioral styles were perceived. I saw that they were expending vast amounts of energy just on survival, and it was hindering performance.

When people are in the midst of change and consciously adapting their behavior, the price is an energy drain. Constantly shifting gears and adapting to new situations tires people out. In light of this we decided to conduct behavioral and values

assessments on the employees, along with individual and group consultations and communication workshops. We soon identified several key employees who were tired and drained, both emotionally and physically. One such employee, "Sean," stood out.

Sean was naturally relaxed, patient, consistent, steady, and unhurried. His unique characteristics included a need for closure and a secure situation. He was also a great listener and planner with the ability to calm and stabilize others. At the same time, Sean was independent, had a strong desire to learn new things, and wanted to share his knowledge in support of others. His ideal environment was one in which he could operate within the confines of a structure that had clearly defined boundaries.

Contrary to his natural style, Sean was in a high-risk environment that required him to handle multiple tasks in a chaotic atmosphere. The environment was "highly-charged" and extremely competitive. His need to be consistent, detail-oriented, and focused on supporting others toward clearly stated goals was stifled. The characteristics and demands of his position were alien to his natural style. There was no question as to why Sean was tired. He was focusing his energy on survival. He was feeling pressure and confusion because he did not know what to do. There was an internal conflict going on because he wanted to be all things to all people.

As we continued to talk about his needs, wants, values, mission, and goals, he discovered that there was a time in his life when he enjoyed doing other things, namely providing training sessions for employee work teams. Considering his inner drive for knowledge and self-fulfillment and his desire to support and help others, this aspect of Sean was not surprising. Unfortunately, he was placing his energy into an entirely different focus. Being in a "survival mode" was unproductive, exhausting, and frustrating.

Sean is a perfect example of someone who is "stuck." When the pain gets great enough and crisis develops, people can no longer tolerate the discomfort of their so-called "comfort zone." They need to restore their energy in positive and meaningful directions. As Sean developed clarity about the values and attitudes he was passionate about, he realized that he was in the wrong job and environment. Ultimately he left for another career that involved corporate technology training. In this new environment he was able to flourish by doing the things that he loved and was best suited for. We'll discuss later more about energy flow and productive ways of utilizing our spiritual energy that will enable us to transform ourselves.

EXERCISE:

Draw two columns: "What I want more of in my life" And "What I want less of in my life." Use this information to gauge your energy level as you determine the things that energize you and the things that do not. Then develop a strategy as to what you need to do, how you are going to do it, and when.

Chapter Five

Determine
Your Needs

"There is only one corner of the universe you can be certain of improving, and that's your own self."–Aldous Huxley

B eing able to identify your needs is the key to getting them met. And when you can communicate those needs to others, they will assist with fulfilling them as well. Your needs are important to know, satisfy, be proud of, and be responsible for, whether they be needs of love, touch, time, or space.

As mentioned previously, the source of every addiction is an unmet need. For example, if someone has a need to be loved, admired, and respected, that person may choose to fulfill that need in a dysfunctional manner rather than in a healthy way. Compulsive shoppers may buy things for themselves to feel love and admiration. This behavior serves as a quick fix "ego remedy" rather than a sustaining manner in which to fulfill oneself. The down side is the obvious high monetary price a person must pay to fulfill the need in this manner.

When needs are unmet, people will strive to get what they want any way possible, even if it involves manipulating others. Unfortunately, this behavior often results in confusion, fear, and embarrassment. People begin to feel resentment towards others because of the actions taking place. Finally, a sense of anger or resignation can result from the situation. The chaos of unmet needs makes it increasingly difficult to "live in the present." It becomes a reactive situation instead of a proactive one.

When you identify and resolve your needs, you feel a sense of clarity and satisfaction that sets you free. And as your wants decrease, your energy focuses in the right direction, and

your life becomes more effortless. To put it another way: fill your cup first, and then you have something to give.

FULFILLED NEEDS CAN LEAD TO GREATER HAPPINESS

Research indicates that security and survival are the two most important things to the human brain. A sense of purpose or a feeling of importance, coupled with a craving to be appreciated, are important for all people to be happy. Getting your needs met in a positive manner is vital as well. While you can ask others for help when necessary, you and only you are in control of getting your needs met. It is not anyone else's responsibility to ensure that.

As you fulfill your needs, it's important to realize precisely what you can emotionally handle and what you're willing to pay to meet your needs. A good example of this behavior is "Karen," a woman who left one relationship for another. At the time she needed a feeling of security and the comfort of knowing that someone was there for her when she was not feeling well. She also identified a need for validation. Her newfound relationship fulfilled those needs quite satisfactorily; however, she discovered that the price of having those needs fulfilled was too high. The relationship was high maintenance and left little energy for her to go forward with her life, maintain her own identity, and follow her mission.

Knowing such vital information about yourself is critical for your growth and development. Relationships that are solid and grounded are ones that evoke a spirit of mutuality and love. They are about having the freedom and support to become the person you want to be. A true partnership exists when you can experience a sense of zest and vitality versus emotional drain or intensity, a sense of freedom with yourself and others, and a sense of confidence and self-assuredness respecting each other's individual genius and passion. A partnership is truly a place where you experience a sense of worth and a connection to the other person beyond that relationship.

It is important to develop relationships that represent strength and fortitude. This is why everyone must identify their needs and wants in a relationship and find ways to get them met. Too often people settle for dysfunctional relationships because they are needy. They end up sacrificing rather than compromising.

Specifically why people stay in unhappy relationships has much to do with having a platform to complain, a place to control, and finally a place to be a caretaker. Rather than use our energy to take care of and fix ourselves, it seems easier to blame others and not focus on ourselves because there is pain involved in becoming accountable and responsible. In reality, the pain of being stuck is no different than dealing with our own shortcomings and finding the strength, courage, and conviction to use those dark moments for our own evolution. Convenience and comfort zones are not lasting or growthful. There is a price to be paid, and all too often the price is high.

THE POWER TO FULFILL IS WITHIN

Situations we encounter in our lives are part of a larger design or purpose. We are here on this earth to learn and grow by helping each other and ourselves. We are each given the seeds we require for our own awakening, and how we view the events in our lives has a lot to do with how we will succeed. Often there are basic needs that are missing in our own growth and development that stem from our past. Think of these as "missing vials." If a person has insecurity from the past because he or she has been abandoned, that person may have a need to control others for fear of future abandonment. These kinds of relationships signify the necessity to identify negative patterns and conditioning and to clean up the past issues or baggage because they will only serve to hurt people.

The fact is that needy people can be repulsive and require tremendous energy. Being with a needy person is high stakes, and it calls for sacrifice instead of compromise. In these situations, identifying and understanding your needs is most

important. When your needs are integrated with who you are, then you can comfortably take care of your wants.

QUESTIONS TO PONDER:
- ♦ *What are my clearest needs at this time?*
- ♦ *How can I get them met? And, when will it happen?*

EXERCISE:

Identify 10 personal needs from the definitions to ponder list below. Then circle one word from the coresponding sublist that best describes the feeling you want to receive from getting that need met. Your completed list represents the values that support your beliefs and creates your standards for being EnlightenUp(ped)!

DEFINITIONS TO PONDER

Appreciation -
(Praised, Thanked, Validated, Valued)
Acceptance -
(Acknowledged, Included, Praised, Respected)
Accomplished -
(Achievement, Fulfillment, Successful)
Cared For-
(Attended to, Embraced, Supported, Treasured)
Communication-
(Care, Clarity, Commitment, Listened To, Share, Talk)
Comfortable-
(Abundance, Luxury, Abundance, Work- free, Served)
Control-
(Dominate, Manage)
Freedom-
(Autonomous, Adventure, Discovery, Independence)
Loved-
(Cherished, Esteemed, Intimate, Touched)

Needed-
(Giving, Important, Useful)
Peace-
(Balance, Calm, Harmony, Steadiness)
Power-
(Authority, Challenge, Lead, Results-oriented)
Recognition-
(Celebrated, Noticed, Seen)
Safety-
(Cautious, Secure, Stable, Vigilant)
Work-
(Career, Industriousness, Responsibility, Sense of Purpose)

What can you do to get these needs met without paying a price that's too high?

Once you define your needs and design a system to get them met while establishing boundaries to make them happen, your goals will then be in alignment with your values and you will accomplish them with the least amount of effort.

CHAPTER SIX

SET
BOUNDARIES

"People are always blaming their circumstances for what they are. The people who get on in this world are those who get up and look for the circumstances they want, and if they can't find them, make them."–George Bernard Shaw

Setting up personal boundaries is the key to creating a problem-free environment. While creating boundaries may sound like a selfish thing to do, it is an imperative part of taking care of yourself. Creating boundaries is about developing a system that prevents others from hurting or harming "who you are," namely, your soul, spirit, or being in any way, whether it be through criticism, screaming, or yelling.

When you create boundaries, you take a preventative measure against physical or psychological abuse. With physical abuse the body can bleed; with psychological abuse the mind can bleed. Preventing either of these scenarios from occurring takes courage, conviction, and persistence to create a safe place environment for yourself. It is a statement about what others are not allowed to do to you.

An example of creating boundaries is telling someone, "Don't criticize or yell at me." Another example is telling others they are not allowed to make demands upon you and suggesting that they instead request, advise, or recommend. Boundaries such as these are a resounding "NO" and a safeguard against the offensive behaviors of others. Tolerating overbearing behaviors from others can cause you to feel numb after a while. This, coupled with not having the skills to communicate what you need, becomes a double-edge sword.

When your boundaries are set, you can effectively spend your energy in more productive ways. Realize, however, that

boundaries are not about controlling the other person; rather, they are about how people need to be in your presence. When you create strong boundaries, you are working toward creating an environment that limits and potentially eliminates the intrusion of others on your time, energy, and space. At the same time there is an opportunity to enjoy the freedom of having more energy and reserves.

THE BOUNDARY CREATION PROCESS

Creating boundaries is the "How to" behavior that supports the "Why" of your values. It also assists you toward creating a platform to align the "What I want" of your goals with your values, beliefs, and needs. And so, when your boundaries are in place, you can get your needs met. As you raise your standards and create boundaries, you simultaneously raise the conduct you live by. This conduct is reflective of your inner strength and enables you to make strides toward excellence. It's what compels you to live by credos such as, "I don't give advice unless asked" or "I don't raise my voice."

As this process occurs, the flip side of boundary standards becomes true as well. For example, if you feel it is inappropriate for another to give you advice or speak to you in a loud tone, then you need to consider it inappropriate for you to do the same. Therefore, it is important to be mindful that boundaries and standards work both ways. Equally important is to choose boundaries you are comfortable with and to find positive role models to emulate. As you learn your part, allow it to integrate fully into your true self.

To set boundaries effectively, you must understand a four-step process. The four steps are Informing, Requesting, Demanding, and Leaving. To understand how these four steps work, consider the following example: One morning at work you are standing at the coffee machine with some co-workers and discussing some last minute changes on a project that your team has been diligently working on for the past few weeks. Just as you are thanking your co-workers for their dedicated efforts and commitment to the project, your boss approaches.

Ignoring the others present, he begins to chastise you for the type font and page layouts on the rough draft you delivered to his desk earlier that morning. As he continues to berate you in front of others, he inadvertently admits that he had not even read the report as yet. Your boss then abruptly turns on his heels and walks away without waiting for a response. You are left embarrassed and humiliated both for yourself and for those who had worked so hard on the project.

You return to your office, take a deep breath, and decide how to handle the situation. You are determined not to lose your temper or act in a rash manner, and at the same time you realize that you must effectively set your boundaries. After careful consideration of the four steps of *Informing, Requesting, Demanding and Leaving,* you call your boss and ask if he is available for a brief meeting.

STEP ONE: INFORMING

Upon being ushered into his office, you take a seat facing him and begin the boundary setting process. First, you inform him that his behavior in front of your team was demeaning, embarrassing, and harmful to all involved. You may say, "They have spent weeks of focused energy on the project and for the past two Saturdays have given up family time to ensure that deadlines were met. They are proud of their accomplishments, and attacking an incidental and easily changed component of the report without even assessing the content deflated not only me but also the entire department. I need you to know that this type of behavior is inappropriate and unacceptable. I would appreciate if in the future you would please be vigilant and avoid this type of interaction."

STEP TWO: REQUESTING

Things go along smoothly for a few days, but then a serious lapse occurs. The boss enters a conference room where you and your team are brainstorming on some names for the new product. You are facilitating an exercise whereby people offer random ideas while you write them on the board. The purpose of

the exercise is to stimulate ideas in an atmosphere free of criticism, then go back and build upon the free flowing suggestions.

After your boss enters the room, he stands with his arms folded and gazes over the names being generated. His face contorts slightly and he asks who came up with such stupid suggestions as "Wizard" and "Blowhard." He then shakes his head in apparent disgust and leaves the room. People glance around the room at each other; their energy and enthusiasm have totally dissipated.

You gather your thoughts, excuse yourself from the group, and follow your boss to his office. After you approach his desk, you remain standing and say, "After our meeting last week I left with the understanding that ineffective and demoralizing interventions would cease. Unfortunately, your intrusion and comments during this morning's brainstorming session indicated that we had failed to reach a clear understanding of appropriate and inappropriate behavior. After I informed you of how this behavior violates my boundaries, I am now requesting that you do not do this again. The effects on morale are devastating."

STEP THREE: DEMANDING

Your boss leans back in his chair and snaps back defensively, "It is probably a wise idea for you to think twice before you come into my office and make demands. I earned this position through hard work and managerial skill, and I'm sure you are mature enough to appreciate the fact that I am your boss. Don't push it! The job market is real tough out there."

In a deliberate but controlled voice you respond, "I appreciate the fact you have achieved your position through hard work and dedication and that the job market is tough out there. However, I need you to understand that it is equally important that you respect the fact that I am serious about my career and dedicated to providing effective leadership and support to my work group. Without your respect for my work and the work of my team, you undermine the potential benefits to the company. In light of this I demand that this type of demoralizing behavior stop."

STEP FOUR: LEAVING

As the weeks progress, your boss's behavior continues, and you are finding it increasingly difficult to work in an environment that is not aligned with your needs and values. You are finding it hard to sleep at night and are becoming short-tempered and irritable with family and friends. Through the grapevine you find out the boss is related to the President and that any attempt to circumvent his authority will be thwarted. You feel drained of the enthusiasm you once had for the position and dread returning to the office each Monday morning. Your performance suffers and you determine that leaving is inevitable. The job search begins, and you carefully interview prospective employers to make sure you find a company whose values and ethics are aligned with yours. A month later, after you have had a tour and ample time to chat with enthusiastic and up-beat employees, you reach across the desk to shake hands with your new employer.

SOME CONCLUSIONS AND OBSERVATIONS:

Notice that at each stage you attempted to bring the problem to a satisfactory and honorable resolution. If the boss had accepted your requests and modified his behavior, the situation would have taken a turn for the better, and a stronger more effective relationship would have ensued.

BOUNDARIES VS. REQUIREMENTS

As you set boundaries for yourself, realize that boundaries are not the same as requirements. Boundaries focus on the "don'ts," while requirements focus on the "needs." An example of a boundary is telling your child, "You cannot go out and play today because your room is not clean." On the other hand, stating that same scenario as a requirement would be saying, "I need you to spend two hours inside this weekend so you can clean your room." Boundaries are about setting rules; requirements are about setting up a give and take relationship.

QUESTIONS TO PONDER:

♦ *What are my boundaries, if any?*
♦ *Why do my boundaries exist?*
♦ *What requirements do I have?*

EXERCISE:

Establish boundaries that eliminate others' behaviors that are harmful to you. List creative ways for people to satisfy your needs.

CHAPTER SEVEN

IDENTIFY YOUR VALUES, YOUR VISION, AND STANDARDS

"Freedom consists not in refusing to recognize anything above us, but in respecting something which is above us; for by respecting it, we raise ourselves to it, and, by our very acknowledgment, prove that we bear within ourselves what is higher, and are worthy to be on a level with it." –Goethe

Our personal criteria are the standards or values in our life that support our beliefs. We are constantly either moving toward or away from our most highly valued criteria. I briefly mentioned values in Chapter Two because of the strong correlation between values and beliefs, which together create a strong framework for our personal foundation. This chapter builds on that correlation as you continue to learn how to create the necessary footing or building blocks toward shoring up your personal foundation.

YOUR VALUES AND YOUR SELF

Since we know that values represent the "Why" in our lives, we must now be mindful of the fact that values are not like articles of clothing that you try on and take off. Values are the very parts of our fiber that enable us to see the world the way we do. Because each person sees the world through his or her own eyes, there is no wonder as to why we can each view the same event so differently at times.

For example, let's suppose we are having a high level executive meeting to discuss a recent real estate acquisition. The scenario is to build an exclusive homeowner's association that would comprise of 54 luxury homes. At this meeting we have six executives who will spearhead this project and get it off the ground.

The names of the executives are as follows:
1. Utilitarian, who is interested in the bottom line;
2. Social, who wants to ensure that people will have full employment;
3. Theoretical, who wants to know all the facts and who demands answers to the questions of what, why, how, who, where, when;
4. Aesthetic, who wants to know if the form, balance, and harmony of the project will accentuate the contours of the land;
5. Individualistic, who wants to ensure that this project is the best and will put the association's face on the map; and
6. Traditional, who has specific beliefs and who wants to ensure that this project will lead the group to understand a deeper meaning and value of life as a whole.

As the meeting gets off to a rolling start, conflict immediately begins. Utilitarian is plainly focused on the project's bottom line and the return on investment, while Social only cares about whether or not the project will help people in the area secure jobs. Theoretical chimes in and wants to know all the facts on the project and asks what, why, how, who, where and when questions. Then, Aesthetic, who deals with a subjective reality, jumps in and conflicts with Theoretical, who is logical and wants to know everything. Aesthetic then proclaims to be more concerned with the beauty of the project than Utilitarian's bottom line. Next, Individualistic starts to use power and influence to assert him/herself toward victory. Finally, Traditional states that the lasting effects of the project are most vital and is closed minded about all the other concerns. What a mess!

Do the events of this scenario sound even vaguely familiar? Most people can appreciate and understand the above interplay. The objective here is to enable you to develop an understanding of attitudes and the interaction of each; to know which attitude drives your life, actions, and desires; and to discover how to understand others' viewpoints and be able to interact convincingly by seeing the world through their eyes. You'll discover that a new understanding of yourself and others can add a fresh perspective to the causes of conflict and dissatisfaction. This growth will put you on a fast track toward determining whether or not you decide to change a situation, change your perception of the situation, leave it, or find a way to cope with it.

YOUR DRIVING FORCE

Certain things or activities, such as freedom, adventure, beauty, contribution, creativity, or discovery, naturally interest each of us. They are the "end values," the incentives that propel us toward action and represent reference points that drive, influence, and stimulate our behaviors. We also have "mean values," which are the action steps we take to acquire our end values. For example, if you wanted to acquire better health or security or freedom, you would have your end values in mind. The mean values would be exercise and diet and money.

Unfortunately, when striving to attain end values, many people end up sabotaging themselves and don't even know it. It may not necessarily be their intention, but it does occur. How? When values direct us toward something, we inevitably experience pleasure. When we are drawn away from something, we undoubtedly experience pain. For example, as we seek to avoid the temporary pain of staying on a diet and allow for the momentary pleasure of succumbing to a candy bar, we end up blindly sabotaging and hurting ourselves in the long run. The answer to eliminating this self-sabotage lies in creating a disciplined mindset that is "in control" and that can effectively deal with real issues. In the above example, the key is to take the displaced power from the candy bar and restore it to its rightful place within the person.

When you honor your values, you live a life of integrity, free from addictions or attachments. It is a state when your needs are met and when creating a passionate life becomes your goal. It is these values that drive behaviors and activities to which you are drawn.

To help you get a better understanding of your inner workings, let's reflect on six prominent basic interests or mo-

tives that reflect behavior: Theoretical, Utilitarian, Aesthetic, Social, Individualistic, and Traditional values. The following descriptions discuss the goal of each attitude or value. They also uncover the passions, overextensions, possible stress factors, and ingredients for success in terms of careers or activities that will serve to energize and foster a fruitful life filled with passion, hope, fulfillment, and purpose.

THEORETICAL VALUES
"NOT TO KNOW IS BAD; NOT TO WISH TO KNOW IS WORSE."
AFRICAN PROVERB

People with theoretical values have a goal to discover truth and knowledge. They are passionate about discovering the inner workings of an event, and they feel overextended when they are in a situation where others are ignoring matters of practicality. Factors that create stress for Theoretical people are twofold: 1) an inability to know or discover, and 2) the experience of a subjective reality as it conflicts with their natural objectivity. Theoreticals want to see the research. They ask the where, what, why, who, and how questions. Their intellectual, rational, and objective approach to people and situations ignite a sense of passion toward identifying issues and solving problems.

Ingredients for job success include educational opportunities, training, and seminars. They crave the ability to gain knowledge and have it challenged, the chance to become an expert and display their expertise to others, and finally the opportunity to move on to another area after achieving excellence in a particular field. These people may gravitate toward discernment, discovery, learning, observing, or teaching as they strive toward personal and professional growth and potential. Possible careers include researcher, teacher, engineer, librarian, historian, or explorer.

66

UTILITARIAN VALUES

"Money swore an oath that nobody who didn't love it should ever have it." -Irish Proverb

People with utilitarian values have a goal to determine what is useful. They are passionate about their practical approach to investments, spending or saving, and return on investment. They also exhibit a sense of efficiency as it relates to time and money. Utilitarians are mainly concerned with wanting to know what resources are required and what the bottom line is.

There are two types of utilitarians: 1) the Producer, who finds a way and charts the future, and 2) the Conserver, who protects resources, cuts expenses, and creates something from nothing. In either case, when utilitarians feel overextended, they tend to perpetuate self-preservation in terms of having little or no concern for others and often display "workaholic" behavior. Factors that tend to create stress are wasted resources, such as time, materials, or services, and investments without return.

Ingredients for job success include opportunities to be rewarded for individual performance. Utilitarians thrive in environments where there is accountability, return on investment of time and talent, elimination of waste, and equipment that allows for efficiency, bonuses, and incentives. All these factors encourage growth and potential. These people may gravitate toward accomplishing, contribution, guiding, leading, mastery, stimulating, or supporting. Although possible careers might include sales, management, entrepreneurial ventures or pursuits, the most significant factor is that they invest themselves in a career that they deem worthwhile.

AESTHETIC VALUES

"A wildflower on the mountain tops would not change places with a rose in the garden."
American Proverb

People with aesthetic values have a goal to experience creative expressions and appreciate nature and its environment. They are passionate about having form, harmony, and balance in all aspects of life. They also thrive on a sense of satisfaction, joy in

subjective experiences, understanding feelings of self and other, and self-actualization.

There are two types of Aesthetics: 1) those who are materialistic and appreciate the finer things in life, and 2) those who are non-materialistic and have a proclivity toward the expression and impression of nature and its environs. Both types feel overextended when they are required to function outside of their own subjective reality. Factors that may create stress for aesthetics are the pressures brought about by objective experiences that lack feeling, form, beauty, and harmony in self, others, or the environment.

Ingredients for job success include balance in all areas of life, family orientation, and employment. Successful aesthetics focus on personal growth and development, self-help, creative opportunities, an unstructured environment with a forum for free thinking, and the expression of subjective ideas. These people may choose to deal with environmental concerns and their effect.

While being observant and creative is their approach, it is important to note that balance and creative expression are factors that encourage an aesthetic's growth and potential. These people tend to gravitate toward beauty, creativity, connectedness, experiential feelings, pleasure, and sensitivity. Possible careers might include psychologist, photographer, dancer, designer, or artist.

SOCIAL VALUES

"THE BEST PASSION IS COMPASSION." JAMAICAN PROVERB

People with social values have a goal to eliminate hate and conflict in the world. They are passionate about investing themselves, their time, and their resources towards helping others achieve their potential. Because they have an inherent love of people, they work hard to ensure that the needs of others will be met. Their selfless nature and generosity enable them to project a sense of passion whenever there is an opportunity to assist others in developing their potential, championing a worthy cause, or bettering society.

Overextensions, such as primarily focusing on others or exercising an overzealous fervor toward a cause, may lead to injurious or harmful behavior to themselves and others. Factors that create stress are individualistic behavior or insensitivity toward others. Ingredients for job success include opportunities to help others eliminate pain and conflict in the world, the ability to be part of a worthy mission or cause, and harmonious environments that have an emphasis on handling the needs of people. Exercising these opportunities while knowing that they are making a difference are factors that encourage growth and potential.

Socials tend to gravitate toward awareness, compassion, devotedness, sensitivity, relatedness, and responsiveness. Possible careers include the ministry, social work, teaching, volunteering, or organizing.

INDIVIDUALISTIC VALUES

"Victory has a hundred fathers.
Defeat is an orphan." Chinese Proverb

People with individualistic values have a goal to assert themselves in a victorious cause. They are passionate about attaining and using power and position. Since their primary interest is centered on power and influence, they will often seek leadership opportunities and positions that focus on achievement, alliances, or the development of winning strategies.

Signs of obvious overextensions occur when the self becomes more important than others or when power over people becomes an issue. Stress factors, such as feeling a loss of position or power or experiencing a lack of opportunity or inability to advance, can accelerate distress in these individuals.

The unique aspect of this attitude has to do with the fact that their value does not stand alone. Clearly it needs to drive through another channel, whether it be through Utilitarian with a focus on resources, Theoretical with a focus on knowledge, Aesthetic with a focus on self-help, Social with a focus on helping others, or Traditional with a focus on changing the world. Here is an example of what I mean and how it works: Richard

Simmons, the weight loss evangelist who has high individualistic values, expresses his aesthetic values of self-actualization, balance, and harmony by helping others help themselves. He is a leader and has led a worthy cause while helping millions of people.

Ingredients for job success for individualistics include opportunities to advance and be around leaders and the ability to enjoy the rewards and authority that accompanies their position. These elements encourage growth and potential. These people tend to gravitate toward accomplishments, adventure, domination, influencing, or leading. Possible careers might include sales, management, entrepreneurial ventures, military, or president.

TRADITIONAL VALUES

"BETTER TO DIE STANDING THAN TO LIVE ON YOUR KNEES." YIDDISH PROVERB

People with traditional values have a goal to find the highest value in life. They can be passionate about finding meaning in life, understanding the totality of life and the pursuit of the divine, dying for a worthy cause, converting others, or living according to a "closed" book.

There are two types of Traditionalists: 1) the Evangelist, who connects others and influences them, and 2) the Protector, who is rather rigid and is more of a separatist. Overextensions occur when a sense of closed-mindedness or judgments prevail, or when they would prefer to sacrifice or die for their cause. A factor that can create stress is someone actively imposing his or her beliefs upon them. Traditionalists' interests may reflect unity, order, and tradition. They tend to show concern for what is being done, while wanting the assurance of moving forward.

Ingredients for job success include working within a system of principles and beliefs consistent with their own and feeling that they are part of a mission or cause while personally achieving and advancing. While these elements encourage growth and potential, traditionalists tend to gravitate toward belonging, devotedness, empowerment, energizing, facilitation, instructing, or spirituality. Ideal careers include philosopher, theologian, priest, or inspector.

ASSESS YOURSELF

The preceding information is for your knowledge. Take a moment to think about those values and qualities you have a tendency to gravitate towards. Realize that some qualities can apply to more than one value. This information will help you elicit the criterion that supports your standards, values, and beliefs.

The next step is to rank yourself in relation to each of the discussed values or attitudes. As you do this, place your preferences in order from one to six, with your feelings of intensity going from the highest to the lowest. Therefore, your number one and two values will be strong, numbers three and four will be situational, and numbers five and six will be indifferent.

Your number one value will be your driving value and will be strongly affected by value number two. The situational values are when your feelings can range from positive to indifferent based upon what other priorities are going on in your life. They become increasingly more important as your first two values are met, whereas your last two values reflect feelings of indifference.

For the sake of simplicity, I will relate the following example. Suppose I have ranked my values in the following order: Utilitarian, Social, Theoretical, Individualistic, Traditional and Aesthetic. In light of the above, it is important for me to focus on making money so I can support a worthy cause, whether it be donating to a non-profit organization, providing the highest quality and level of education for my children, or saving for retirement. When I have made the necessary provisions for my children's education, the non-profit organization, and retirement, I may very well want to focus my energy and interests in other areas. As a result, I may become interested in learning something new (theoretical) that has a utilitarian twist, perhaps how to effectively manage financial portfolios. After I have mas-

tered this new endeavor, I may decide I want to share it with others in an effort to make their lives better. So, I decide to draw upon my individualistic values and teach at various organizations or institutions, believing these would be good places to share my knowledge. Now my social values have come into play, as I am working toward helping others achieve their potential. This is a prime example of how situational attitudes can have an effect on your life and how your third value has a tendency to affect what you do in approximately thirty percent of the cases.

By now you should be able to imagine what it would be like if you have low traditional values and are faced with a situation with someone who has that value as number one. Their sense of passion and control could be overwhelming to you, especially if your feelings of indifference are negatively rooted. As you do the following exercise for yourself, you can continue to think and wonder what the driving forces are behind your actions and what they might specifically mean to you in your life.

QUESTIONS TO PONDER:
- ◆ *What are my values?*
- ◆ *What truly motivates me?*
- ◆ *What are my reasons for why they are important to me?*
- ◆ *What changes do I need to make in my life to fully honor my values? For example, do you need to change beliefs or jobs, or let go of attachments?*

EXERCISE:

From the following list carefully select the values in order of priority and rank them from one to six, with one being the highest and six being the lowest. Then determine the following: your two top driving values, your two situational, and your two indifferent values. Take some time to process the information and determine how and why you react to different situations, people, places, or things. Contemplate on how you may want to change the situation or your perception of it, or even decide to leave it or find a way in which to cope with it. Feelings and observation are key ingredients toward developing clarity and awareness in this discovery process.

The six values and the qualities that may relate to those values are as follows:

1. **Theoretical** (Discern, Distinguish, Discover, Learn, Observe, Teach)
2. **Utilitarian** (Accomplish, Contribute, Guide, Lead, Mastery, Stimulate, Support)
3. **Aesthetic** (Beauty, Creative, Connected, Experiential, Feeling, Pleasure, Sensitive)
4. **Social** (Awareness, Compassion, Devoted, Sensitive, Relatedness, Responsiveness)
5. **Individualistic** (Accomplish, Adventure, Dominating, Influencing, Leadership)
6. **Traditional** (Belong, Devoted, Empower, Energizing, Facilitate, Spiritual, Instruct)

Discover Your Vision

Whenever people want to make a change, they need to evaluate three things: their standards, their beliefs, and their strategies. We have already discussed beliefs, and we will cover strategies toward the end of the book. For now, let us focus on standards.

Standards are important for setting goals and are directly related to our vision. While congruent goals serve to push us in the right direction, our vision is what pulls us toward carving a new reality. Your vision and mission encompass your beliefs and values. They reflect your joy, gratitude, and peacefulness in the role you see yourself moving toward. Think about your vision as something to play with in the here and now, giving it the energy it deserves and allowing it to further enrich your life.

A familiar maxim states, "When the student is ready, the teacher will appear." The same is true with a vision. When your life is full, your vision will come. Focus on your outcome as you think about what you want to do for yourself and others.

When this perspective gets big enough, the "how" will appear along with the inspiration, strategies, and solutions. Then it is time to translate your vision into action.

Walt Disney was a man with great vision who encouraged people to dream. He once said, "What I see way off is too nebulous to describe. But it looks big and glittering." Disney's belief in dreams was nothing new, though. In many cultures, "dreaming" is considered an ancient and vital practice. Dreams are a way of building our inner strength as we step into the unknown, expand our sense of believing, and grow into greater beings.

YOUR REALITY SHAPES YOUR VISION

During the course of your life and career, you experience many changes. Each of your experiences has brought you to different places in terms of others, your environment, and yourself. As you journey through life, realize that the Universe makes no mistakes, and you learn lesson after lesson, whether it be understanding sickness and ill health, failed relationships, or career transitions. Life becomes a collection of experiences, while the interchange goes on between human will and Divine Providence.

The paradox of life with the coexistence of things both negative and positive becomes ever more so apparent. As we draw from these paradoxes, develop greater clarity, learn, and grow, we finally see the grand purpose of our evolution. The real issue continually emerges as a need to accept and own "self responsibility." Mother Teresa said it best: "I have found the paradox that if I love until it hurts, then there is no hurt, but only more love."

After "walking in many shoes," our sense of awareness becomes more acute and so does our personal and business mission until it clearly directs us toward the perfect work. During this process, you will undoubtedly feel ambiguity, confusion, or fear that requires courage, faith, perseverance, and tenacity to prevail. However, once you recognize this fact, you allow the formation of your mission to expand and grow.

My personal experience went from one-on-one coaching with an individual client base that included coaches, professionals, people in transition, to company executives. The evolution toward companies became possible as I helped companies grow by developing their people. So often, companies wondered why they would hire consultants to create strategic goals and objectives and then watch the process fall apart within a relatively short time period. It was clear to me that companies needed people to facilitate the communication process as a platform to make their strategy work and ensure that the visions, values, strategies, and goals were in alignment for both the company and its people. Improved communications, effective management skills and techniques, and job compatibility were critical to ensuring productivity and growth for all parties involved.

As I continued to grow during this process, I experienced a need to write as well as teach. These efforts were an extension of my mission, which was consistent toward bringing clarity, structure, and support to individuals and companies who wanted to be productive and develop a sense of harmony, peace, and balance in their lives. It soon became clear to me that there were many people helping others bridge the gap in going from the conditioned self to the unconditioned self. My mission to be a messenger who sends energy to connect my client's truths to one another with a spirit of love, understanding, passion, and adventure felt right.

The bottom line is that as we follow our mission, we become increasingly aware of our own personal attributes and how they relate to what we are doing. In my own experience, I felt I was using my talents to illuminate the way for others in an inspirational and spirited manner. My position with others and myself was focused on, "Ask, and it shall be opened to you." As a result, my personal motto became, "To be yourself and live each day to the fullest." With increasing clarity and awareness, my vision began to appear: "To envision a world of energetic empowerment where people learn to utilize their inner re-

sources toward understanding, appreciating, and becoming one with themselves, each other, and the Universe." The wisdom from this vision spoke directly to my spirit: "Let your heart feel and speak the songs of silence."

As you assimilate this knowledge, allow yourself to understand what the heart knows, couple it with the questions of the mind, and peacefully come to terms with "what is."

QUESTIONS TO PONDER:
♦ *What is my vision?*
♦ *How does my mission project my vision?*

EXERCISE:

As you identify your mission and purpose, now is the time to become even more abstract and contemplate "who and what else." For example, as you defined your mission with a true sense of "who you are," your being found work to fulfill your sense of purpose. Now take some time to explore and embrace your spiritual dimension that is beyond the scope of your material self and identify yourself within a larger system.

STEP ONE:
Sit in a comfortable position and relax. Breathe in and out, and with each exhalation, become even more relaxed. Close your eyes and begin to clear your mind of the day's clutter. As you see, hear, and feel your stress floating away, your mind continues to rest and wander as you create a space for your vision in your mind's eye. Ask your unconscious mind to provide you with creative ideas toward a greater dimension of yourself. As you consider the things that give you pleasure and meaning in your work, play, relationships, community, and personal areas of your life, remember to thank your unconscious mind. Have fun and enjoy your creative self as you contemplate all the possibilities that go beyond your present day existence. Allow your spirit to soar.

STEP TWO:

Remaining in a relaxed state, imagine yourself discovering certain thoughts and sensations as new insights evolve. Ask yourself, "What is it that gives me the most pleasure in my work and in my life?" "How do they relate to my values and passions?" "How does what I do bring meaning to my life and benefit the world at large?" "What are some of the ways I can expand my mission to enhance my living experience and that of others?"

STEP THREE:

Now that you have identified key elements of your being, consider specific actions and behavior modifications that will bring your new vision and mission to reality. Be specific. After developing these action steps, emerge from your relaxed state enthused and determined to make these changes in your life.

CREATE STANDARDS

Once you have identified and communicated your needs and requirements, established boundaries, determined your values, and shaped your vision, the next step is to develop your standards, which are self-made rules to which you hold yourself accountable. Rather than an obligation, standards are choices that become automatic and enable you to live life in a relaxed manner. They are a natural extension of the behavior and excellence that afford you the opportunity to continually grow, develop your higher self, and experience a richer life.

Standards may include how you perform your work, the manner in which you treat people, or even the things you allow in your life. Once you establish standards, there is no more deciding at every turn. You have a definite path to follow and your choices become second nature. Standards are also an expression of your values – the things that are true to you, namely self-care, honesty, integrity, power, commitment, tolerance, reserves, and acceptance. I mention acceptance because when you create your standards, it is critical to be nonjudgmental while

honoring and acknowledging what is present and doing the best work you can by listening and observing.

Some examples of standards that people live by are:

- I am truthful and honest.
- I am someone who is prompt and responds in a timely manner.
- I am someone who respects and honors my body and does not abuse it with drugs, alcohol, or food.
- I am responsible for myself and take that responsibility seriously.
- I am intelligent and committed to lifelong learning.
- I am aware of my strengths and weaknesses and will capitalize on my strengths by doing the things I love and delegating those things that represent limitations.
- I am someone who refrains from taking anything personally.
- I am someone who does not make assumptions.
- I am someone who takes action, lives in the present, and always does my best.

Standards are a personal reflection of your character and set the stage for you to create the life of your dreams.

QUESTIONS TO PONDER:
- ◆ *What are my standards?*
- ◆ *How will they improve and enrich my life?*
- ◆ *How do they express my values?*

EXERCISE:

Slip into the "creative thinker" role and allow yourself the time to dream, think, and feel what comes to mind as you list the standards you live by. Then discover ways to raise those personal standards. Remember, these are extensions of the natural part of who you are and allow you the opportunity to develop your higher self, thus being able to enjoy your life and share the gifts you have been blessed with.

When evaluating your standards, ask yourself the following questions:

1. What is my level of commitment to the things important to me in my life?

2. What am I dedicated to and what are the beliefs that I hold true to myself?

3. What is it I am willing to accept and what is it I am not willing to accept, whether it involves people or situations?

4. What am I tolerating in my life? Are they within my control or not? Do they mean compromising or sacrificing myself? To what degree do they limit my happiness, growth, or healing? What specifically can I do about it, and what is it I am going to do?

5. In terms of my authentic being, what will I do to maintain integrity in my life with others and myself? What are my strengths and limitations, and knowing them what is it specifically I can and will do to maintain that sense of "being in the flow" within my relationships and myself?

6. How can I truly be honest with others and myself? When and under what circumstance does being honest require me to be silent? Perhaps "control" and responsibility issues are at stake here, namely are these circumstances within my control or not, and what specifically is my responsibility in these particular situations?

7. What about exercising my power, enforcing my standards, and preserving my integrity and honesty? Is my power derived from myself or it is from another? Do I use my power to empower others, or do I use my power over others? Lack of accountability or blaming is a sign of giving up my power to change. The more I derive power from within myself, the more reliable my power will be.

8. What about my communication style? Do I communicate in an open, loving, non-confrontational manner? Am I able to listen, actively and passively? Do I acknowledge another by clarifying, paraphrasing, giving feedback, and summarizing content and meaning in an empathic manner? Do I explore options and elicit possibilities, resources, and actions? Do I offer advice when asked and share my point of view? Are my

relationships based on autonomy and mutuality? Am I in a position to give or do I want?

9. Healthy relationships are based on giving. If we are in a relationship to see what we can get out of it, it will not work. Am I whole in terms of myself to be in a relationship whereby I will use it to construct myself and grow and not impose my model of the world on another?

Getting to know and understand yourself are key elements of personal growth. As you determine what your mind, body, and spirit require to feel satisfied and balanced, you learn how to elevate yourself to a new level while maintaining high standards with integrity.

You have the ability to get in touch with this inner place of peace and creativity. As you tap into this resourceful state, you become aware of new thoughts and sensations. You may begin to wonder how this information will integrate. Realize that the answer to this question is already within. As you continue on your journey, the answer will present itself when you are ready to discover it. This, I can promise.

CHAPTER EIGHT

CREATE RESERVES THAT ENHANCE YOUR LIFE AND IMPROVE YOUR EFFECTIVENESS

"I am the master of my fate:
I am the captain of my soul."
—W.E. Henley (Invictus)

In order to stop going from one miserable situation to another, you need to create reserves within yourself. When you create reserves, you invest in yourself and create the space in which to attract what it is you want in your life. You develop a feeling of having more than enough in terms of the extras that allow you to be comfortable while you experience less stress and enjoy a "place of integrity."

Some examples of reserves can be elements of self, time, space, money, freedom, love, attraction, energy, wisdom, support, and opportunity. A basic example of not creating reserves would be buying new clothes for a closet that is already full. Where will you put the new clothes? Sure, you could force them in the closet, but doing that would only damage the existing clothes and cause your new clothes to get buried in the midst of all the old clothes. On the other hand, if you create the space by cleaning out your closet (essentially creating your reserves), then you will have room for the clothes you both want and attract. The same holds true with relationships. It you want a fulfilling relationship in your life, clean out the relationships that do not work, create the space for another, and it will come.

Clearing mental reserves is no different. In fact, it is vital to clear your mind and create space by doing a crossword puzzle or taking a walk. Sometimes the chatter of the body "ego" mind is quite distracting and prevents "that good old intuitive feeling" from entering.

And finally, consider energy reserves. Healthy foods stimulate and work toward the long-term preservation of creating self reserves with healthy mental, physical, and spiritual states, while junk foods provide the quick fix stimulation and hinder the process. The same holds true for positive beliefs versus negative beliefs. Positive beliefs increase energy and create reserves of self with better mental, physical health, and spiritual well being, as well as time in terms of being proactive and productive. In addition, they contribute to your overall feelings of having a restored sense of balance, peace, and harmony. Negative beliefs create a feeling of "being stuck" as they block and drain energy, ultimately affecting your health and life.

Make a conscious effort to clean up areas of your life, whether they be physical, emotional, mental, or negative belief structures. Work on healing wounds and freeing yourself from drug, food, or alcohol addictions. The idea is to determine what is draining you, minimize the drain, and fill your reserve cup. Having strong boundaries and standards enables you to become more centered, focused, and attractive while at the same time they naturally create the space for reserves.

As the process continues, a profound shift takes place with regards to boundaries and standards. Initially, they enable you to form a strong foundation and identity; however, as you grow, you place less emphasis on boundaries and standards because your foundation is already in place. The boundaries and standards become more automatic since they have already been melded into your evolved self.

The process of creating reserves reminds me of a client named "Heather," a bright and sensitive young woman, recently divorced, who was struggling emotionally, physically, and financially to make ends meet. In order to survive she held two jobs, one as a dental hygienist in a hospital during the week and another as a medical aide for an elderly patient on Saturdays.

About a year after the trauma of her divorce, Heather met a young divorced man with two small children. Over a brief period of time, the two developed a serious relationship. "Tim," who had custody of his two young children, ages 4 and 6, had enormous responsibilities and was struggling to find a balance between work, fatherhood, and childcare needs. Heather, being the caring and sensitive person she is, responded and pitched in four nights a week with preparing dinners, laundry, baths, and lunches for the children. In addition, Tim began placing increasing demands on Heather with respect to entertaining his family and occasional friends with the little time she had left.

As she kept up this schedule, Heather was losing more and more weight. While the chaotic lifestyle she created for herself provided a temporary escape from the problems she had been avoiding, the new unhealthy situation was creating a progressive toll on her. The adrenaline that had kicked in for so long started to burn out.

One night after keeping up this grueling schedule for over eight months, Heather was driving home and hit a deer. Not only was her car extensively damaged, but she also ended up hospitalized with serious internal injuries. As she lie in bed, for the first time she was unable to run away and had to deal with the painful issues she could no longer escape. At that point, desperation set in, and Heather made a responsible choice to seek psychological counseling to help her cope with her issues surrounding love.

One of the coaching exercises Heather worked on was quite revealing. She drew two columns. The first was titled "What I want more of in my life," and the second was titled, "What I want less of." To Heather, the revelations were astonishing. The correlation between the columns was significant enough to show her that it was time to take the suggested extreme self care she was both consciously and unconsciously crying out for.

Heather's columns revealed that she wanted more time, money, love, energy, self-esteem, and health and less stress, chaos, debt, fear, fatigue, feeling of worthlessness, and sickness. The results of this exercise plus assessments on Heather's values and style were quite telling. First, there was an epiphany when Heather realized her strong social values needed an adjustment. Her primary focus on helping others had become in-

jurious to herself. Heather needed to first love herself before she could give love to others, and in order to do it appropriately she needed to create sufficient reserves of love. Heather then realized that the demands of her current relationship were no longer appropriate. Over a short period of time, that relationship became history.

With continued counseling and coaching efforts, Heather began to develop a real relationship with herself. In addition, she discovered that her strong technical skills and capabilities could be brought into other career areas within the hospital that would pay more money. As one of these positions opened up, Heather applied for a job as a lab technician, took a short-term training program to give her the additional skill sets required, and got the job. Now she was on a roll and feeling a good sense of responsibility and control over her life.

Self-love, which initially was an alien feeling to her, began to take hold. Her feelings of fear, worthlessness, fatigue, sickness, and debt began to dissipate as she took action toward shoring up reserves of self-esteem, time, and money. As a result, Heather's focused choices gave her a renewed sense of freedom and energy to continue upon the road to good health and positive relationships with herself and others.

CHOOSING THE RIGHT DIRECTION

By channeling your energy in the right direction you are using time wisely. As a matter of fact, when shifts occur in your life, you often create reserves simultaneously. Let's look at the attitude shift example from earlier: "I am someone who is health conscious, and I will experience better health as a result of limiting my intake of fattening foods." Because of your new commitment to staying healthy, you will experience less sickness and be more efficient, productive, and free. Because you're spending less time dealing with illness, you have more time reserves. In addition, being sick less often also helps conserve your money supply. You will feel better about yourself, love yourself more, and feel more attractive and energetic.

To sum it up quite simply, think of it this way: When your needs are satisfied, you experience a level of comfort and more reserves of energy and vitality. When your values are honored, you experience a stronger connection with your own power and source. And when your vision and mission are clear, you avail yourself to more opportunities and life keeps moving ahead.

QUESTIONS TO PONDER:
- ♦ *What are the reserves I want to create for myself?*
- ♦ *How will I achieve these reserves and when?*

EXERCISE:

The following exercise builds upon the one we did in Chapter Four. For the purposes of this chapter, the exercise will take you further to help you understand how to create reserves that will enhance your life and improve your effectiveness.

First, draw two columns. Title one: "What I want more of in my life." Title the other: "What I want less of in my life." Observe the two columns and ask yourself if it is possible that you are not having the kind of life you want, need, or deserve because of the correlation that exists between the two columns.

For example, suppose you want more money to support an extravagant lifestyle, and you want less stress. What would happen to the stress if you had more money? If this is relevant, then stress no longer becomes the issue, and the focus becomes money. Your choices then become: "What do I have to do to get more money and not feel stress," or "What can I do to simplify my life and eliminate stress?" Once you make these internal alterations, decide what type of reserves you want to create. Then ask yourself the following questions:

1. Is there anything else that I want more of that can possibly be the cause of what I want less of?
2. What specifically might they be?
3. What reserves do I need to create to enhance my life and improve my effectiveness?
4. What are the ways that will enable me to create these reserves?
5. How will I achieve these reserves?

CHAPTER NINE

SET COMPELLING GOALS

"If a man would move the world, he must first move himself." –Socrates

When you control the direction of change, you incorporate your needs, wants, and aspirations to achieve your desired outcome. The key to this step is to identify goals, which project the "What I Want" aspect of your being. Your wants are important, as they give you a sense of purpose and serve to motivate you. When your activities and work are aligned in the same manner, you become congruent with "Who You Are." Then, the fulfillment, gratification, and feeling of motivation toward seeking more challenges enhance your continuing desire to be creative and innovative.

Moving in this direction requires you to change. Unfortunately, most people are afraid of change. The reasons why are plentiful. Some people don't want to change things in their lives because it would upset the comforts they currently enjoy. Others get mileage out of being where they are because it becomes a way to create intimacy with others.

Whenever change occurs, there is always a trade off, and the fact remains that it is normal to experience grieving over the sense of loss that change often brings about. However, goals serve as motivators and allow us to set the direction of change. When you are in control of yourself, your life, and your destiny, you experience a feeling of goodness that paves your way toward competence.

THE PURPOSE OF GOALS

Goals give us the opportunity to evaluate what we are doing, make choices, and develop clearer insights and awareness of what we want to be, do, and have. They also help us identify

what boundaries are necessary for us to achieve our highest potential. Because our goals compliment our mission, our sense of purpose, and our sense of who we are and what our needs, wants, aspirations, and desires are, it is imperative to set goals based upon what is best for you and not by what others deem important. On a personal and professional level, setting goals reduces stress and confusion and increases control, motivation, and productivity, thus enabling us to enjoy a healthier immune system and sense of inner peace.

As you begin to set goals, understand that there are many different facets to life that are important to your self-development in order to maintain balance. In fact, your personal value system governs behavior in three areas: Organizational, Professional, and Personal. These areas need to be in alignment with each other for inner peace and spiritual balance to occur.

The question then becomes, "How do I do this?" First, take each area and determine your own values. For example, the Personal Area may serve to identify strategies that relate to Spiritual, Family, Physical, Social, Intellectual, and Work. The Professional Area may serve to identify strategies that relate to Image, Customer, Employee, Compensation, Growth, and Product. The Organizational Area may serve to identify Growth and Innovation, Financial Performance, Customer, Employee Relations, Productivity, and Image. You then segment these strategies into areas that take on the life of a goal.

To utilize this process, try this mind-mapping exercise. Draw three different circles with each behavior in the center: Personal, Professional, and Organizational. Around each center, draw lines or boxes that represent the strategic elements of Spiritual, Family, Physical, etc. Use these areas to select the goals you want to list under each area. When writing down your goals, be mindful of the fact that there are short-term (one month or less), intermediate (one month to one year), and long-range (one year or more) goals. This is important to know because you may want to work on them in stages, beginning with short-term goals and then advancing to intermediate and long-term goals.

Before you begin to list your goals, take a look at the key elements to setting goals and creating a balance in life.

♦ Shoot for attainable goals that are harmonious with one another. For example, if my intellectual goal is to read two books per month, perhaps I may want to join a book club as a social goal.

♦ Maximize the benefits and minimize the pain. Realize that your goals do not need to be focused on pain. Suppose I wanted to lose weight. I can accomplish this goal by eating in moderation and exercising rather than by totally depriving myself.

♦ Focus on the journey, not the end result. Life is a process, not a destination. All things happen in their own time and space sequence. Sometimes we need to release the struggle to try to make things happen and look at our growth as a process that is continually evolving with an outcome in sight rather than a destination.

♦ Happiness is not always what you want. Be flexible and open to change and modification. Can you recall a job or home that you desperately wanted at one time and felt great disappointment at not getting it? Was the next job or home even better than what you could possibly ever have imagined?

♦ Enjoy yourself, have fun, and most important, learn from the past, live in the present, and work and plan toward the future.

Life is an adventure, a challenge, and an opportunity to grow and connect with others in a special way. Living it with a sense of enthusiasm, passion, desire, and commitment enables you to soar beyond your wildest dreams.

SCHEDULE YOUR DAYS AND YOUR GOALS

As you set your goals, assess your values, and organize your timeframes, schedule various days of the week according to your goal timeline. Categorize each day as either a Spiritual, Buffer, or Work day. Doing this will enable you to deal with the "big picture" and at the same time stick to the present and be

comfortable. Here's how the process works: Spiritual days represent total relaxation. You are entitled to do nothing or do something. It's totally up to you. Depending upon how you are feeling that day would determine your direction for the next 24 hours.

On the other hand, Buffer days are for learning new skills and cleaning up house, namely doing paperwork, returning phone calls, etc. Finally, Work days are purely intended for income-producing activities. Based upon your needs you can determine how you want to organize your time and then modify it accordingly depending upon what your goals are.

QUESTIONS TO PONDER:
- ♦ *What goals do I need to help me achieve my potential?*
- ♦ *Are these goals in alignment with my values?*

EXERCISE:

1. List five goals you want to accomplish. They can be either short-term, intermediate, or long-term goals.
   - ♦ Road Test
   - ♦ Jeep
   - ♦ Dentist
   - ♦ Job
   - ♦ Doctor

2. List five values you hold true to yourself.
   - ♦ loyalty
   - ♦ honesty
   - ♦ family
   - ♦ health
   - ♦ morals

3. Match your goals with your values. If your goal does not fit with one of your values, either adapt the goal to fit the value, get rid of the goal, or come up with another goal. Do not adapt your value to the goal. As you do this exercise, ask

yourself what is the specific benefit of the goal. For example, if your goal is to lose weight, then the benefit would be to look and feel better, be healthier and fit, and have lowered blood pressure.

4. Prioritize your goals.

5. Plan your goals.

Use the SMART Model for Goal Setting to plan how you will accomplish your goals.
The following steps will guide you.
S: Be *Specific.* State your goal in specific terms, determine the outcome, and describe a specific action you will take. Example: My goal is to lose five pounds in three weeks.
M: Make it *Measurable.* As you define your accomplishment, set a specific time whereby you will know when you have accomplished the goal and what the scope of the change is. Example: Three weeks is measurable for a five-pound weight loss.
A: Be sure the goal is *Action Oriented.* Identify what you will do, develop a plan, and find a role model if necessary. Example: I will call a weight-loss support group and schedule my initial appointment for May 1st. I will attend two meetings a week for three weeks and continue for another month to learn how to effectively maintain my new weight. In addition, I will exercise three days a week for 30 minutes each time.
R: Make the goal *Realistic.* Your goal should be consistent with your abilities and convenient for you to do. However, remember to be flexible and initiate change if necessary. Example: My weight loss goal is realistic, and I have scheduled an appointment for May 1st to hold myself accountable.
T: Make the goal *Time-Bound.* Be certain that your established timeframe is within reason. Example: I will begin on May 1st and continue for a total of seven weeks, which includes maintenance.

6. List the necessary action steps under each goal.

CHAPTER TEN

PATHWAYS TO ENLIGHTENUP

"The heart is the only compass that can direct you on the long journey to inner peace."–Glen Ridless

Both your internal and external resources create your future. As you embark on this next phase of your journey, you need to develop strategies that foster, nurture, and support your spiritual transformation. Think of these capabilities as your tool kit for success. In this chapter you will learn resourceful methods and techniques, such as knowledge, skills, tools, and language, that affect your belief structures. How you decide to utilize the tools in this kit helps you define more effective ways to deprogram your conditioned self while adopting new ways toward becoming your greatest gift – the gift of yourself. You can create a new level of awareness that can be pivotal in your spiritual transformation. This process allows you to see the world through different eyes.

Using a metaphor to expand on this concept, think about your world as a map. Now think of the world outside of yourself as the territory. The map is what you see. It is an illusion. The territory is what you don't see. It is reality. Life gets easier when you embrace reality. When you escape reality, denial sets in and you deplete your energy reserves.

Strategies provide new directions that serve a greater purpose. They can be used to interrupt negative emotions and provide a course of action. For example, a feeling of disappointment is not a sign that the world is ending. Rather, it is a time that we need to let things be and accept the fact that "this too shall pass." During this time, questions such as "Is this an unrealistic or concrete expectation of mine?" are vital. A reality check is to explore your belief system and work toward the real issues one at a time.

93

Before we get into specific strategies, let's first become aware of and understand some significant feelings such as resentment, anger, frustration, and fear. As we explore these emotions, let's be mindful that the answers to personal growth do not lie in repressing or expressing them in harmful ways, but rather to experience them honorably. The opportunities for personal and spiritual growth lie in working with and through these emotions as we learn how to open up, heal, and protect ourselves at the same time. There is no doubt that the process can have a powerful impact on how we view ourselves, others, and situations.

EXPLORATIONS OF FEELINGS AND EMOTIONS: RESENTMENT, ANGER, FRUSTRATION, FEAR

Resentment may surface when we do too much to be nice, which results in one person over-functioning and another under-functioning. This is an unhealthy situation for both parties. When feelings of resentment occur, it's a time to define your "self" responsibilities and control, and it is important to cherish it as a signal to enjoy yourself more and do less.

Resentment is not a joyful experience, and when joy is lacking, sorrow is present. During these moments, you may experience feelings of distrust and the need to distance yourself, ultimately fulfilling a self-rejecting prophecy. This is common because resentment falls into the house of sorrow, whereby perceptions of experiencing life as a gift are blocked. Instead, the feelings of being righteous, judgmental, prejudiced, and angry lead to self-rejection because you lack the need to be loved or appreciated.

Clearly, there are times when resentment is justified because we are being exploited. In these situations, it is imperative to set boundaries that will honor and restore you while supporting the growth of yourself and others. There are also times when we may need to take a leap of faith and love without expecting love in return, give without wanting to receive, or even hold without being held. In these moments it is important to find the discipline to take a leap of faith and allow yourself to experience trust and gratitude instead of distrust and resentment.

Anger is a conflict between what is and what you want. It fosters a feeling of not being in control and having expectations and judgments that create negative emotions and feelings. Anger is really about loss. What is it you feel you have lost? Is the loss justly founded, or is it something your ego has created? What does your ego think it is lacking or what do you feel a strong compulsion or desire for? When these feelings occur, your personality feels weakened and threatened, resulting in a form of anger, hurt, or resentment. Often times it is the very essence of this anger, which is founded in the ego and based in fear, that prevents us from getting the love we want. It separates us from having and experiencing what we are so deserving of.

For example, suppose you woke up one morning and decided you would enjoy a day off from work. As you go through the process of imagining the emotion, you create the desire, and this desire turns into a need that begins to take on a life of its own. You can actually taste and feel what a day off would mean to you. As the ego continues to stoke its fire, you go through the motions and call your boss and ask for the day off. When your boss says no, you may chose to get angry because it is something that you really felt you needed at this point. Your ego has created an expectation that has you believing this is what you need now, not later. This is what happens when we concede to the wants of our human personality that focus on expectations, which become the root of our problems, rather than to the needs of our spirit.

As you can see, the ego has great power and is usually behind the reason why we sabotage ourselves. Our intention is not to harm ourselves, but to avoid pain. In reality, it becomes a self-created problem with the expectation that the ego set up to satisfy its false need. It really is a sense of experiencing mixed signals.

Remember, the ego is part of our psyche and is a power unto itself. It is concerned with the outside world and exists for

a reason: we need the ego to grow. The idea is to control it with discipline and be able to distinguish between a real need and a false need the ego creates. It is about being congruent with your mind and heart. If those parts are not in agreement with each other in terms of identifying what their positive intention is with effective strategies or options that are congruent, then disparity predominates and a person's energetic spirit is in a different place.

Anger can be a growthful emotion when used to your advantage. It clearly has a purpose. For example, if someone abuses you, you get angry. This gives you an opportunity to communicate your feelings, free yourself from pent up emotions, and learn how to forgive the person and not the action. Anger will serve its purpose by enabling you to set a boundary so that the abuse will never happen again.

The idea is to rationalize the anger, let it go, and come to terms with understanding your needs, wants, beliefs, behaviors, and values. When you understand these parts of yourself, you are in a better position to understand the roots of your anger and deal with it effectively.

The best way to deal with anger is to use "I" language to communicate your feelings. For example, suppose someone always interrupts you when you speak. Instead of confronting the person by saying, "You are so rude when you constantly interrupt me," take the steps to place the blame on the action, not the person, and communicate your feelings in "I" statements. Say, "When you interrupt me (name the action), I feel angry, hurt, and disappointed (name the feeling), because the behavior is inappropriate, unacceptable, and not a kind or caring manner in which to treat people (name the reason and belief)." This takes the negative energy away from the person, addresses the offending behavior, and clearly states your feelings.

When you are able to communicate effectively and define whose issues belong to whom, the next step is to visualize "letting go" as you see, hear, and feel the behavior going off into the distance. Statements such as, "I have no control over this person or situation; I did not create or cause it," are important to resolving this feeling and moving on. It helps to bring clarity to a situation that needs diffusing. Most important, remember to be mindful that difficult and challenging situations are for our own growth and that they serve a purpose.

There are two interesting perspectives on the common tendencies of how we express our anger. Some people let out anger by yelling at someone or something. Let's put these people in the category of "yellers." Other people say nothing and keep their feelings inside. We can refer to them as "stuffers." Neither tactic works because those people are not fulfilling their needs, namely to feel better, stay connected to the person who upset them, get an apology or an explanation of what the hurt was about, and avoid feeling guilty when they express or don't express themselves in such a manner.

By remaining silent we feel worse because we are not dealing with the source of our anger nor will we be getting the hoped for apology or acknowledgment. On the other hand, when we yell, we think we are in control when we really are not. And when we push others away, we feel guilty afterwards.

So what is the best approach? Remember to express your angry feelings in a clear manner using the "I" language. Using this approach enables you to feel better emotionally and physically because you are using your own power to assert control over the situation. In addition, you are dealing directly with the source of your anger, avoiding any unnecessary guilt, and are more likely to get the understanding from others and perhaps even an apology.

Frustration occurs when you want something now and are impatient for the results. At this point, it's important to remember that it is not your will but God's will that needs to be done. Being impatient only creates problems for yourself. Letting go of your expectations and attachments and surrendering and readjusting your belief system can serve as a way to release frustration and bridge the gap over your impatience.

Fear is a negative emotion that can sometimes be lethal when it distorts false evidence or expectations as appearing real. Fear represents separateness, where lower values are based on dishonesty, mistrust, self-interest, competition, secretiveness, control, and hidden agendas. Rather than bring out the best in us, fear has a way of bringing out the worst. Blaming, judgments, criticisms, and defensiveness are all externally machinated manifestations of the ego that surface when fear is present.

Love and fear often go hand in hand. Humans want to be loved, and when they do not feel loved or if that need is threatened, they lose faith and fear surfaces. Fear can result in manipulative tactics, anger, hate, revenge, frustration, resentment, and other diabolical behaviors. Ironically, the things we are most fearful of are often the things we attract in our lives. It is far better to change our fears to concerns by reframing them (discussed later in this chapter) and using the known cure of "faith" as a spiritual path.

POSITIVE TRANSFORMATIONS

Clearly it is time to utilize some spiritual strategies to focus on the positive emotions of love, generosity, connectedness, discipline, and enthusiasm. Love is a feeling of being connected, open, aware, and accepting. Generosity is empowerment and giving to others, while connectedness is a oneness with God – a feeling of gratitude, acceptance, and a safe place. Discipline is having the sense and determination to want to feel, look good, learn, and shore up a foundation for growth and empowerment. Enthusiasm is the ability to enjoy what is in the present and feel joyful in having a positive self-esteem along with a sense of gratitude, good fortune, and the desire to explore. Higher values based on love focus on a sense of community and fosters honesty, integrity, trust, common good, cooperation, openness, participation, and individuality.

In addition to the exploration of your feelings and emotions, evaluating your belief system and your expectations, judgments, control, and responsibility issues is an integral part of your spiritual journey. Faith and spirituality go hand in hand and are representative of the core of our highest self – the pure God-like nature of love that comes from and resonates from our hearts. As we tap into our spirituality using our spiritual toolbox of beliefs to explore, define, and refine ourselves, we learn a new language that is paradoxical to our human beliefs.

As our spiritual beliefs help us deal with our own humanity, we develop a transformational sense of growth and understanding. This renewed sense of empowerment enhances our personal and collective mission because when we make the slightest difference in the world on an individual level, the geometric progression continues to serve the "whole" of humanity. Thus, our individual and collective missions, which are focused on helping each other, are also helping our individual selves as we continue the transformational process of growth and creation. Acquiring the real essence of "who we are" instead of "who we have been conditioned to be" is a lifelong process focused on achieving our highest potential.

The ultimate criterion necessary to acquire this quantum leap of growth that defies the "conditioned human self" is the development of a belief system that personifies the "unconditional spiritual self." This system of principles and beliefs focuses on self-responsibility and accountability and reflects a pure love that is truly representative of who we are spiritually.

While our spiritual journeys are a reformative and transformational process, the developmental and evolutionary growth heightens our awareness of appreciation, gratitude, trust, obedience, compassion, servitude, and joy. It becomes a path of choices when it comes to beliefs, value commitments to ourselves and others, behavioral patterns in life, and the way we practice our faith. As we deepen our relationship with God, we become more enlightened and empowered to a dynamic force that is within us and beyond us at the same time. It is a force that is vital to helping us achieve our truest identity, meaning, and purpose.

The other parts of the process include:

√ Resolving blockages;
√ Understanding the elements of change;
√ Developing a mission statement with a compelling vision;
√ Focusing energy in positive and useful directions;
√ Defining needs;
√ Eliminating tolerations while securing boundaries;
√ Determining values;
√ Raising standards;
√ Creating reserves;
√ Identifying goals.

Having accomplished these tasks, a natural momentum begins to take shape in the form of a critical mass where resources and synchronous events come together and pave the way for you to become irresistibly attractive. As a result, opportunities begin to come to you. When a major shift of this proportion occurs, people tend to be happier because they are more fulfilled, and life begins to unfold in a most extraordinary manner. SunTzu, Chinese Warrior/Philosopher, Fifth Century, takes it a step further when he states, "Opportunities multiply as they are seized."

QUESTIONS TO PONDER:
♦ *What are the areas and situations of my life where I feel resentment, anger, frustration, and fear?*
♦ *How do I deal with these emotions?*
♦ *How can I deal with them more effectively?*
♦ *What does spirituality and faith mean to me?*
♦ *What are the spiritual principles and beliefs that foster a sense of responsibility and accountability within myself?*
♦ *How do these beliefs serve to guide me toward achieving my truest identity, purpose, and meaning in life?*

TOOL BOX ESSENTIALS

Now that we know precisely which emotions and feelings we are battling, let's examine the various strategies that can enable us to *EnlightenUp* and achieve a sense of inner peace and oneness with the Universe. Realize that every technique won't work for every person. The goal is to understand the following strategies and utilize the ones that best fit in with your life. By incorporating one or more of these actions into the steps you've already taken, you achieve a greater sense of connection to everything around you.

RELAXATION: YOGA, MEDITATION, EXERCISE

Yoga means "union." It is a healing meditation in motion that establishes and supports a harmonious connection between the mind, body, and spirit. The practice of yoga aims to remove all restrictions and conditionings of the mind that cause separation with others or within ourselves. For example, when the ego-mind projects false fears, the same body-mind reacts to these falsely perceived threats with a high priority.

Yoga uses the breath to awaken "Prana," the intelligent spiritual energy that the universe is made of. It is the *"qi"* or "life force" that resides in each one of us. The various yoga poses serve to awaken and free the Prana from the ego mind, remove the blockages, and carry out physical, mental, and emotional purifications. It is about learning how to use this transformative, intelligent life energy of Prana for our own health, healing, personal growth, and spiritual evolution.

The benefits of yoga are both internal and external. Internally, yoga serves to strengthen the mind through attitude and positive intention. Externally, yoga works through the body in terms of form and technique. Yoga is a way to transcend the mind by overcoming its limitations and achieving a higher level of consciousness as we awaken ourselves to our own perfection.

Meditation is an ancient practice that brings us to a place of oneness and presence of God. The Bhagavd Gita tells us: "The

101

practice of meditation frees one from all affliction; this is the path of yoga. Follow it with determination and sustained enthusiasm...." This translation emphasizes the experience of wisdom and peace and gives affirmation to meditation as a peaceful state that is achieved through using the breath, a mantra, or motion in the form of a walk.

There is a distinction between the mantric and breath forms of meditation. With mantric practice, one tends to "tune out" and become oblivious to any external stimuli, whereas with breath meditation, the effects are quite different. Instead of "tuning out," the voice becomes muted and sounds are heard but are not bothersome. This is an especially efficient method of relating from a quiet state. It could be compared with the Biblical metaphor that you are "in the world, but not of it"—a peaceful place to be. It is an effortless state where insights, feelings, and images appear spontaneously.

The key to accessing this Life Force and activating healing is for the breath to be deep, slow, quiet, and regular. This gives you a chance to explore the silence that is the true foundation of your being – a "safe place" where you can clear your mind, listen, observe, and feel restored. When you experience a level of deep rest in meditation, your body has the ability to release stress and purify itself. A deep stillness sweeps over your whole being and removes you from the daily life events that continually surround you.

During meditation, visualize the energy system in your body, better known as the "chakra" – the place from which you derive your sense of balance and consciousness. The issues that you deal with in your life get stored in these centers and block your energy, causing both physical and emotional pain. You can use meditation to access and alter these energy centers through the use of color.

As you begin your meditation, either sit in a chair or lie down. Slowly breathe in and out, relaxing more and more with each breath. While you are breathing and relaxing, allow your mind to wander and experience different sensations. Imagine yourself seeing a rainbow, with each color of the rainbow likened to each chakra of the body. Breathe in and visualize the red color of your first chakra, which is located at the base of your spine. As you see, hear, and feel the color of the rainbow streaming through your own chakra system, allow this powerful energy to heal, enlighten, and empower you.

As you become aware of these sensations, you can continue to explore and discover new learnings that will enable you to become more at peace with your mind, body, and spirit. You can listen to the sounds of your inner voice as it guides you toward the happiness you are so deserving of.

This meditation teaches you how to best use the phenomenal power of this visualized energy and transform any negative physical energy into positive energy. In the above example using the first chakra, you put your attention to a place where issues of fight or flight exist. Placing your attention on the various energy centers in this way is a worthwhile exercise that will help you direct your power away from negativity and alter your state to a positive one in which you can become more congruent with your inner truths.

For the purposes of completing this meditation, the following explains the remaining energy centers. The second chakra, orange in color, is located approximately at your lower back or hip level and deals with creativity and sexuality. The third chakra, which is in the solar plexus, is yellow and deals with issues of personal power. The fourth chakra is green and near the heart. It is the place where we experience love. The fifth chakra is at the throat. It is blue and deals with self-expression. The sixth chakra, located in the mind's eye, is indigo and represents vision. The seventh chakra, violet, is the spiritual center and is located at the top of the head. It focuses on dealing with present time.

Meditation grants you a sense of alignment with your mind, body, and spirit. It provides a sense of awareness and enlightenment that everything at this moment is happening now and it is right, thereby empowering you to enjoy the assurance of inner and outer congruity. By taking the time to center your-

self on a regular basis, you can gradually strengthen the influence of Spirit in your life and weaken the thousands of ego-based distractions that visit each and every day. This is more than learning how to relax. Rather, it is a restorative process that provides you with the guidance on learning how to live.

Exercise is vital to your well being. It serves to balance your whole system, mind, and body. Exercise gives more energy than it takes. A simple walk, for example, allows us to shift gears and nurture the present in a mindful way and clears our head of all the difficulties of the day. At the same time, exercise helps us experience better digestion, elimination of impurities, healthier muscle tone, clarity of thought, and increased energy. Exercise is an outlet that is required for us to take better care of ourselves and experience a release from the mundane routines and pressures of our daily lives. When you hook into the type of exercise that motivates you, your endorphins get going and you feel your best.

QUESTIONS TO PONDER:
♦ *What relaxation techniques work best for me?*
♦ *How do they improve the quality of my life?*

MANAGING YOUR STATES
Everyone has two states: mind and body. Mind refers to the questions you ask yourself and others. Body refers to your voice, facial expressions, posture, and breath. Managing your states has to do with your behaviors, how you feel about yourself and others, and how you believe others perceive you.

Keep your mind positive by asking the right questions, namely "What" and "How" questions instead of "Why" questions. For example, ask yourself, "What does this mean?" or "What should I do?" rather than "Why did this happen?" "Why" questions denote dead-end answers and usually lead to little resolution or action.

Your body can also enable you to feel positive. Studies have shown that people communicate through gestures 55% of the time, tone 38%, and words 7%. With this information in mind, understand that your voice has different intonations, your face has 80 different expressions, and a standing tall posture identifies your state to yourself and others. Essentially, your motion creates your emotion.

Your breath is vital to your state as well. The more oxygen in your system, the fewer toxins. Breathing also serves to stimulate the immune system and improve cell communication. Consider your Breath and Spirit as one and the same. It is your Higher Self. Each and every one of us has been given the gift of this energy that enables us to go into our inward journey and use our intuition or intelligence to seek higher levels of performance. Later we will discuss how to use this powerful resource as a way to be in the moment, make a conscious choice about what it is you are holding on to, and let it go.

It is not surprising to witness how deeply rooted some of our experiences and reactions are to our body's posture. Have you ever noticed how animals tend to react to people who show aggressive postures and expressions? I recall the story of a friend who had adopted a dog. Every evening when my friend came home and greeted the dog, the animal would have "an accident." After much frustration, he decided to take the dog to a vet, who said that the dog was most likely intimated by my friend's manner. The prescription was to come in the door, not look at the animal, and speak in a soft voice while reaching out and gently petting the dog. It worked! The dog responded well to the positive posturing and that was the end of the problem for both.

As for myself, many years ago I began experiencing back problems and went to a physical therapist for treatment. As we discussed the course of treatment, he observed my standing posture and made some suggestions on improving it. I immediately changed the way I stood and sat. Shortly thereafter I noticed a shift in the way I was feeling, both emotionally and physically. I felt a newfound level of confidence and assuredness, a feeling of strength, and a sense of happiness.

As I was experiencing these changes, I thought of a time when I had gone to a Shakespearean play and found myself

mesmerized by one of the players. The actor took on various roles that displayed several different emotions. As his facial patterns changed, so did mine. The intonations in his voice told me so much about his states, and in some ways, the words he was saying made no difference because his gestures, tone of voice, posture, and breath said it all. When it comes to the mind and the body, it is important to understand the power behind your expressions and to know that you can change your emotions simply by changing your physical state.

QUESTIONS TO PONDER:
- *How am I managing my mind and body states?*
- *What effects are my states having on my life?*

VISUALIZATION

Have you ever had a dream that someone was chasing you, and then you suddenly woke up and found yourself lying in bed with your heart racing? That is the power of visualization. Because the mind cannot tell the difference between what is real and not real, visualization works for many people.

One visualization strategy that is quite powerful is to establish various points in a room that will invariably access a specific resourceful state you may want to experience when addressing certain situations. This is similar to athletes visualizing their course of competition and seeing themselves successfully experiencing every moment from start to finish. If you have ever observed some of the Winter Olympic downhill skiers at the starting gate, you can see them using this visualization technique. They are indeed running the course in their minds, and if you carefully tune into them, you can even notice their subtle body shifts as they navigate the imaginary hairpin turns.

In your own life, you may want to visualize health and well being, or even visualize the ingredients of a successful person. As you visualize, use positive affirmations to support your mental images. It is best to keep your affirmations in the first person and in the present. For example, "I am a self confident, enthusiastic leader with flexibility who attracts success in personal achievements, business, and relationships." Use the SELF acronym to remember the ingredients that create successful visualization:

S Self-Confidence: If you like and believe in yourself, others will do the same.

E Enthusiasm: The inner electricity transmission.

L Leadership: People want to be led. Five percept of the population lead the remaining ninety-five percent.

F Flexibility: Work is continually changing.

QUESTIONS TO PONDER:

♦ *How could visualization help me?*

♦ *In what areas of my life would visualization be most helpful?*

MODELING (RESTRUCTURING SELF)

Modeling is about restructuring yourself. It is a chance to polish and create a personalized stamp of yourself. For example, if you choose to be successful, then you must emulate success. Think of a table with legs. The tabletop is your belief that says, "I am successful." Each leg denotes a specific support of that belief, such as "act successful," "dress the part," "feel the part," and "believe the part." Equally important is to find role models to help you learn how to deal with the part. Realize that it takes approximately 28 days to create a habit. Use your belief as an affirmation and repeat it 15 times a day for 28 days. At the end of this time, you will own a new belief. As you create new belief systems, be mindful of your mental and emotional states and use them to capitalize on newfound beliefs.

Modeling also includes surrounding yourself with people you care for, while you commit your life to something bigger than yourself. During this time, it is important to focus on the support and nurturance of your family and friends, while you look toward the community for personal fulfillment and a place with shared values that enable you to continually grow and be challenged. As you continue to restructure yourself, you will

find places to utilize your gifts to make the world a better place. This is a chance for you to "walk your talk," while leaving your gifts as a legacy to all.

As I began to grow and change and open myself to new ideas, insights and knowledge, I picked out various role models and selected those qualities that I felt would bring out the best in me. I then used visualization techniques and imagined myself in a more resourceful state. Soon I noticed a change beginning to take place in me, and at the same time, in some of the people in my life. There is no question that we are all connected and we affect one another in more ways than one. The dynamics of our relationships have a lot to do with the evolution of people and their affects upon one another. Have you ever been told that someone wanted to emulate you? Or, have you ever witnessed someone trying to emulate you, whether it be in behavior or even dress? How did it make you feel? Life is about evolving and growing, and as you encounter life's situations, you realize that you are here for the purpose of loving and helping others to be the best-evolved self they can possibly be.

QUESTIONS TO PONDER:
- *How could I use modeling to restructure and improve my self-concept?*
- *Who would I choose to model?*

REFRAMING

Reframing means restructuring the situation or event. Have you ever been in a situation that was literally painful? The pain of that situation may have created negative feelings that caused you to lose control and temporarily damage your self-image. Often our self-concept is at the heart of stress-related disorders. To alleviate this, we can expand our model of the world and open our minds to see things differently. Regardless of the circumstances, you do have the ability to see things in a new way or a new context. While stepping back to look at things from a wider perspective or a different angle, you can become more aware of how you see the truth of various situations.

To begin the reframing process, ask yourself the following five key questions:

1. What is good about this situation?
2. What's not perfect yet, presuming that it can be perfect?
3. What am I willing to do to deal with this situation?
4. What am I not willing to do in order to deal with this situation?
5. What do I need to do in order to make the best of this particular situation?

These questions will enable you to effectively communicate and identify the unwanted behavior, determine what the positive intention might be, create alternative ways to behave, and come to terms with new choices.

These questions will also give you clarity. Questioning enables people to develop a solid sense of the situation along with an understanding of what needs to be done. As they go through the question and answer process with themselves or a facilitator, they often discover inner resources to deal with the events and then realign themselves using those newfound resources. This self-realignment helps them deal effectively with the situation, delineate issues of responsibility, and take promising action steps.

So often we find ourselves in situations that we need to get through, whether it be a commitment that we have made, a one-time job that we promised another without realizing the impact of our involvement, or the stress of being in the midst of a job change and wondering where we will be relocating. Attitude has much to do with how well we persevere through these situations, especially since attitude is something we are in charge of. The fact remains that life is 10% what happens and 90% how we react. Thus, our attitude determines how we will do what it is we need to do. We cannot change our past or the fact that people will behave in a certain way; however, we can reframe our situation and develop a different point of view that will enable us to deal effectively enough to relieve our anxiety and enjoy the benefits.

Albert Einstein had the right idea when he said, "There are two ways to live your life. One is as though nothing is a miracle. The other is as though everything is a miracle." As you discover ways on how to change your perception, the following viewpoints will serve to expand your worldviews and put them in a different light. Thinking, looking at, and feeling as though situations are challenges instead of obstacles puts us in a "can do" frame of mind. Viewing the cup as being half full instead of half empty ignites a sense of optimism with renewed energy and gratitude. And finally, if we ever find ourselves in a "reactive" mode, we can always remember to take the "c" out of "reactive" and put it in front of the "r" as we find ways to become "creative." Combining the above strategies with an attitude of gratitude is a power-packed formula for reframing any given situation.

A friend of mine recently told me of the following technique that has been quite instrumental in helping others restore order in their lives. It's called The Suitcase Theory, and it is a technique that serves as another way to reframe multiple situations that can be unsettling or overwhelming.

When we think of any given situation, there are various components that are important to human beings in order for them to identify and put things in perspective, namely qualifying, quantifying, restricting, and shipping out. So when you have a host of challenging situations, qualify the problematic issue or challenge, quantify it, restrict it to an imaginary suitcase, and put ship dates on them.

For example, consider the scenario of a husband and wife going through a divorce. Naturally, they feel as though their whole world is coming unglued at the seams. The Suitcase Theory enables them to make the first step and take appropriate action toward ensuring security and stability. It is a way of putting things in perspective and giving people a greater sense of clarity and hope, while learning to live in the present and surrender without attachments or expectations.

The steps for this divorce example are as follows:

1. Qualify it: The couple understands what they have to do and takes action by ensuring the lawyer does his/her job and gets all the issues in order.
2. Quantify it: They determine the length of time the divorce will take, say approximately 9 months.
3. Restrict it: The situation, along with the husband or wife, gets assigned to a suitcase.
4. Ship it: By putting a ship date on the divorce of April 15 (or whatever the divorce date is) the couple can work toward closure.

This exercise gives people the resources to deal with the complexities of life and enables them to experience a sense of freedom and hope. They then have the ability to focus on the issues of the day and on what has to be done next.

QUESTIONS TO PONDER:
♦ *What situation or event in my life do I want to reframe?*
♦ *What techniques would work best for me?*

LAUGHTER

Are you looking for a stress reliever, increased immune cells, an instant face-lift, a unique form of exercise, or another way to connect with yourself and others? Then laugh to your heart's content. Studies indicate that laughter lowers levels of the stress hormone cortisol and helps to regulate blood pressure, heart rate, and mood-elevating beta-endorphins.

A good belly laugh is known to be a fun and effective internal jogging exercise, as well as a way to minimize feelings of anger, hostility, aggression, anxiety, and depression. When we laugh, those released endorphins are the very chemicals that trigger the emotions of joy and ecstasy. These emotions enable us to experience a resounding sense of inner joy and bliss and establish bonds with others. How sad it is that research studies have indicated that a four-year-old laughs 400 to 500 times a day, while the instances of adult laughter drop down to 30 or less times a day. So go to comedy clubs, rent your favorite comedies, observe children at play, or perhaps even adopt a pet. Observing some of the antics of a child or puppy can truly be

hilarious and heartwarming as we are drawn closer to the inner joys of the experience and the ensuing relationships.

QUESTIONS TO PONDER:
- ♦ *Have I laughed today?*
- ♦ *What are some of the things that make me laugh?*
- ♦ *How can I invite more laughter into my life?*

BEHAVIORAL PROFILES

Think about the following statement: "All behaviors are adaptive in the context in which they are learned, and each and every behavior has a benevolent intention at its source." This may be an unusual concept to grasp intellectually; however, instinctively, it is easier to understand. For example, imagine a salesperson who is well educated, technically knowledgeable and experienced, skillful at his or her job, yet lacking the interpersonal skills necessary to succeed. While the job requirements state that this person must have technical expertise, most important is the person's ability to solve problems in a collaborative manner and influence others to his or her point of view. Achieving the latter aspects becomes a difficult task when the person's self-esteem is low, and abrupt and insensitive behaviors become a form of self-protection. These people get locked within themselves and feel as though they are not being listened to. When this happens, the job becomes increasingly difficult. Is it their intention to turn others away? Not particularly; however, people often treat others as they have been treated themselves.

All behaviors are patterns we emulate from the role models we have had in our lives. They are ritualistic in nature in terms of the ways in which we see the world. Outsiders often take our behaviors literally. Therefore, the key to understanding behaviors is not to interpret them in a literal sense. When we do, problems arise as a result of conflicting values and beliefs.

Eliciting behavioral styles and values are important because they provide complete pictures of people and how they respond to situations, namely the actions they take and why.

The importance of this information lies in the fact that often times peoples' behaviors are not subject to change if they are against their values; however, intelligence can serve to modify their behaviors. The question then becomes: "If people are not aware of how they act, then how can they intelligently change their behaviors?"

This knowledge enables people to manage themselves toward success because people learn how to meet the needs of a majority of people. In order to be able to identify those needs, you must be able to learn how to identify different styles within yourself and others. For example, according to Target Training International, Ltd., there are four different behavioral styles: Dominant, Influencing, Steady, and Compliant, better known as DISC.

The Dominant style is ambitious, strong-willed, decisive, determined, competitive, and adventurous. These extroverted people need to direct and dominate others. This task-oriented individual has high ego strength. Their goal is to handle problems and challenges in an active and aggressive manner while gaining results with little or no fear. Under stress, this person may display impatience or emotional anger.

The Influencing individual is convincing, enthusiastic, poised, and social. These extroverted people need to interact with others and influence them to their point of view. Their strength lies in their ability to be optimistic, trusting, and people oriented, while their goal is to have social recognition. Under stress, this person may experience disorganization.

The Steady style is passive, deliberate, stable, predictable, and non-demonstrative. These people are introverted and need to serve others. This people-oriented individual's strength is in being a loyal team player with a desire for wanting results. Their goal is to experience traditional practices with a slower pace. Under stress, this person may display possessiveness and resistance to change while remaining non-emotional.

The Compliant type is logical, analytical, cautious, systematic, and exact. These people are introverted and need to comply and follow the rules and regulations set by others. This

person's strength is one of accuracy and being highly intuitive. Their goal is to do things the correct and proper way. Under stress, this individual may be overly critical and experience the emotion of fear.

The purpose of knowing this information is to first identify your own style, recognize and appreciate the behavioral style of others, and then learn how to blend and adapt your style to win in any environment. Learning how to interact and communicate in the style of others allows you to experience their sense of reality. When you can understand what people need and want, and then use the appropriate words and language, more meaningful communication opens.

PROFILES IN ACTION

One day I was working with an individual client, and while we were discussing his behavioral style and values, he mentioned that his wife often complained about his listening skills. She often felt that he ignored her and did not always hear what she was saying. Through questioning, he discovered that his communication style was to fix and present solutions rather than listen to what the other person was saying and focus on how to collaboratively solve the issues. Needless to say, this had a negative effect on their relationship, because his wife's needs of wanting to be listened to, understood, appreciated, validated, and respected were not met. He soon realized that her underlying need was to be understood, while his need was to "fix." As a result, they both shared these new insights, worked on closing the gap, and enjoyed a renewed relationship with a more solid foundation.

Another individual, who was well aware that he grew up with a sense of detachment, felt threatened when someone would touch him or come into his space. As we began to discuss different styles and values within the group, he began to understand that people were not aware of how he was feeling. Together, we found strategies on how he could deal with people coming into his space without feeling intimidated. At the same time, the dialogue, facilitation, and sharing enabled other people

114

in the group to develop an awareness of how he might be feeling under those conditions and what actions they could take to understand each other's differences.

Effective feedback focuses on improved communications, both intrapersonally and interpersonally. Adapting our behavior to a given situation is a conscious effort. And when we are in a situation that requires us to consciously adapt our behavior to an extreme, the long-term result is an energy drain that leads to burnout.

JOYS IN DIVERSITY

As individuals develop an appreciation for themselves and an understanding as to what their strengths and limitations are, they tend to trust and work with those who seem most like themselves. Yet, by learning how to adapt to the style of others, you can find ways to gain and experience a greater sense of commitment and cooperation from a greater variety of people. Understanding how to blend and adapt with different people allows you the opportunity to offset your strengths and limitations with others. In this way you can effectively capitalize on your strengths and work toward being the best you can be individually and collectively. The extra dimension to this effort is the profound benefit of experiencing a different point of view as you expand your model of the world.

An old adage says, "Relationships can be our greatest pain and our greatest joy." The ongoing challenge is to communicate in a style your listener will listen to and understand. Paving the way to gain commitment, cooperation, and trust is an effective way in which to resolve and prevent conflict and deal with issues of diversity. As you experience life in many of its forms and variations, it would behoove you to be mindful that the strength of America lies in its diversity. It is the soil of our success, and the ways to overcome diversity are to listen, understand, confront situations in a respectful manner, and then effectively communicate to make a successful transformation.

YOUR PERSONALITY USER'S GUIDE

It's important to remember that all people are unique and need to be supported in a way that capitalizes on their uniqueness. Each of us possesses gifts, which are a manifestation of the talents, skills, and abilities that make us special. Besides being unique, we are all on purpose and have what I call "self asset/ resource" management, meaning every individual is his or her greatest asset. We all have the resources to capitalize on our assets and make them the best they can be. Understanding our own profiles allow us the opportunity to discover precisely how to optimize our tools.

The combination of tools and coaching creates a powerful dynamic directed toward changing the self and putting energy where it belongs. Giving individuals the necessary guidance and support helps them develop a sense of clarity and awareness about who they are, and what they want to be, do, and have. However, clarity and awareness mean little unless you take action and move life in a forward direction. This is when structure comes in. Structure represents the tools that an individual needs to act on, namely management tools to know what it is they have to do in order to manage, motivate, coach, communicate, and develop themselves in a work related environment.

The last part of the equation is a support system in the form of one-on-one consultations, seminars, or communication cluster groups where there is an ongoing process to discuss obstacles, challenges, opportunities, and other pertinent issues that need to be dealt with. This supportive function is crucial since it enables people to have someone providing external support while they are building inner strength. It is precisely this type of support that sustains performance.

QUESTIONS TO PONDER:
- ♦ *What is my behavioral style?*
- ♦ *Are my behaviors getting me the results I want or are they standing in the way of my success?*

East Meets West

The Tibetan view is that every human being is a potential genius. They believe that if you cultivate your abilities, creativity, insight, and understanding, there is no limit as to what you can do. Similarly, the Buddhist view is that human beings have unlimited potential, and the primary mandate of human life is for all humans to cultivate their power of wisdom, justice, gentleness, love, and creativity to a maximum degree.

On the other hand, the Western view is that human beings are intelligent and have a reason for everything. Their life's path is in relationship to an external God, and as people mature and become more conscious, they become more God like. By combining Eastern and Western philosophies, you can enhance your purpose in life. When you open up your power of understanding and awareness and utilize the strategies in this book, you can create a healthy belief system that supports this heightened consciousness and growth.

Understanding Your Greater Vision and Turning it into Action

The following is Diltz's Model of *Vision Into Action*, which is an adaptation from Bateson's neurological model. It describes the correlation of how identity, meaning, and purpose come together.

The function of each level is to synthesize, organize, and direct interactions on the level below it. For ease of understanding I will discuss the flow from the bottom up and then relate how it all comes together from the top down.

First is the Environment level. These are the external conditions upon which a person reacts or behaves. Here we have the constraints and opportunities that answer the questions "Where and When."

The next level is the Behaviors that tell us how we respond to our environment. They are the actions we take and answer the question "What." The behavioral instrument discussed earlier interprets emotions and needs. Our behaviors are needs motivated, which are influenced by our beliefs and values.

Capabilities are the internal and external resourceful strategies, communication tools, and techniques that guide our behaviors to deal with our environment. It's about direction and perception and serves to answer the question "How."

Beliefs and Values answer the question "Why." Values are the driving force of motivation that help us denote our passion. They are incentives that propel us into action because they stimulate and drive behaviors. For example, if a graduate student wanted to go back to school, values would indicate the reason why. The person could be returning to school purely for knowledge, for personal power, or to make more money. The answer could be one or more or all three. This awareness of why we do the things we do and how we behave is important to understanding ourselves.

Mission has to do with our identity. It's the "Who Am I." Mission is about our role or sense of purpose. Here is where we consolidate the whole system of values and beliefs into a sense of self. It is not unusual to discover that here is where blockages exist.

Finally, we have Vision (beyond self). It's the realization that we are part of a larger system. Vision can be elusive if we don't take care of ourselves first. Often times when our vision is clear, the strategy to reach it appears. It is the attainment of a spiritual level in terms of having defined your true essence and envisioning the big picture. Having belief, intention, and commitment is the powerful combination that enables us to encapsulate the totality of this model. In so doing, we go beyond our selves while becoming congruent in mind, body, and spirit.

Now let's take a look at how this all flows together. First, beyond self is the spiritual aspect of us. The vision of allowing ourselves to experience an added dimension of our self gives us a renewed sense of purpose and identify with a mission based upon our beliefs and values. These are the elements that motivate us and give us permission to employ internal and external resource capabilities that regulate our behaviors in such a way as to how we relate to our environment.

As changes occur at the top of the model, they filter down with renewed meaning. Learning to go beyond self is about spending more time in the "other" than in the "self." The process focuses on learning how to deal with diversity, how to grow through the challenges it presents, and then how to view the world not by our individual map, but by the territory that lies outside of ourselves.

QUESTIONS TO PONDER:

- *Are there areas in my life where I am feeling confused, or stuck?*
- *Do I want a change in my life and I'm not sure what direction to take?*
- *What specifically are these areas?*

EXERCISE:

As you go through this exercise, be as creative as possible. You could use the Reframe technique by asking yourself Five Key Questions at any time you deem appropriate. For example, let's pretend you are dissatisfied with your job. You know in your heart it is the wrong job, and you need to look for another. You want to get another job; however, something is holding you back. Here's how the process might work.

PREPARATION:

Before addressing significant issues in your life, it is extremely beneficial to prepare yourself by employing the various tools described in this chapter. For example, relaxation techniques utilizing the breath will enable you to effectively manage and align your body and mind states as well as help you visualize a clear picture of what the desired outcome will be using modeling and reframing techniques. These resources will free your mind of the daily clutter and enhance your creative genius. Also, seek out the humorous components of virtually every human situation. Laughter is an extremely potent stimulant.

STEPS:

First, tap into your emotions and confirm how you are feeling. Unhappy? Tense? Fearful? Stuck? Then ask yourself, "What is stopping me?" "What am I afraid of?" "When I think about changing jobs do I get scared because I am afraid of taking the risk and possibly failing?" Once you have elicited the issue, you can proceed to work through the limiting belief. Here are the initial steps:

1. Identify your Present State, the Gap (Issue), and Outcome (Goal). For example in this case it might be that your Present State is one of being stuck with a feeling of fear and anxiety. The Gap is your limiting belief that reflects your fear of perceived consequences and unmet needs, and the Desired Outcome is to move on to a stimulating and rewarding job.

2. Convert your fear to a concern and ask yourself these Five Key Questions as they relate to the issues of the present job you want to sustain while you're in the process of making the change, or use them to challenge the limiting belief. For example, the results might look something like this:
   - What's good about this situation? *"The discovery and awareness of my limiting belief."*
   - What's not perfect? *"The pain of feeling stuck, restricted, and restrained."*
   - What am I willing to do? *"Explore my belief, work through it, and change it."*
   - What am I not willing to do? *"Hold on to my limiting belief."*

- What is it I need to do to get me through this time? *"Define the process as* it relates to the following questions."

3. Then ask yourself the following questions:
   - What happens when I believe this way? *"I am stuck in a bad place."*
   - What do I accomplish by believing this? *"Nothing."*
   - How does this belief make me feel? *"Miserable."*
   - What am I thinking, seeing, or hearing? *"It is time for me to break through this barrier?" "I see no future in this place." "I hear the frustrations of my inner critic."*
   - Why is this change important? *"It will free me up to have a more rewarding and meaningful life."* (Note: Freedom becomes the criterion that will be pivotal in your growth.)

4. Generate a new empowering belief and proceed to ask yourself:
   - How will this new behavior change serve or benefit me?
   - What would it look like, sound like, feel like?
   - How will it affect other areas of my life?
   - How will I know I have it?

ACTION PLAN:

Once you have completed this exercise and have clarified your Present State, The Gap, and your Desired Outcome, create a Personal Action Plan. For example, decide what specific changes will support your changed belief. What do you need to do more of and less of? Decide when you will begin.

As you formulate your future direction, remember to consider your behavioral and values profile. Then set dates for the completion of an effective resume, identify resources for finding a new job (i.e. placement agencies, newspaper ads, industry journals, networking contacts, etc.), and set up initial interviews. Schedule a target date for starting your new job.

Keep the action plan handy and constantly refer to it as you work through the process. Regardless of what the challenge is, utilizing this technique will help ensure a positive outcome.

CHAPTER ELEVEN

THE LANGUAGE
OF SPIRITUALITY

"When you are joyous, look deep into your heart and you shall find it is only that which has given you sorrow that is giving you joy." –Kahlil Gibran

Your language reflects your beliefs, expectations, and attitudes. When we speak of language here, we're not referring to language as in English, French, Spanish, German, etc. We're talking about the language of spirituality, which is the by-product of your belief system and that personifies your truest essence—love. The following reflects what can happen when you change your language.

Your beliefs, expectations, and attitudes change as your perception changes, and in so doing the dynamics of your relationships change as well. People will respond differently to the altered behavior you exhibit. For example, if you are more caring, people tend to become more open and responsive. Likewise, if you are negative, people will pull away and become more aggressive or hostile. Essentially, what you put out to the world is what you will receive back.

The language of spirituality is centered on commitment, trust, the common good of all, cooperation, openness, and community. When people focus on this spiritual language, they change their assumptions, which in turn changes their behaviors. When they change their behaviors, they change their life. This is a wonderful correlation. Let's now take a look at some examples of language and the profound effect it can have on our lives.

THE LANGUAGE OF FORGIVENESS

Forgiveness is the selfless act of placing your energy in a forward direction. Spiritually speaking, forgiveness opens your heart, which in turn opens your mind and your perceptions.

Opening our minds and perceptions requires an understanding of how we close down, namely with judgments, biases, attitudes, and beliefs that limit our potential. These judgments create separation, rejection, and violence that lead us into a less resourceful state and escalate our preoccupation with hurt, anger, resentment, and fear.

Many people tend to limit themselves with self-boundaries; they state likes and dislikes, create black and white distinctions, and believe in good and bad thinking. These limitations stem from belief systems that manifest "weak egos," which clearly serve to lessen our enjoyment of life. Of course, on the lighter side, there is great truth in Oscar Wilde's comment, "Always forgive your enemies; nothing annoys them so much."

Although I feel that life's purpose is to love, I am also strongly committed to the idea that forgiveness comes first. When you think about it, forgiveness touches every aspect of our lives. In every successful relationship, forgiveness is an ongoing practice. Without it, there can be no communion between people. Instead, old wounds continually surface, causing hidden resentments, negative thoughts, and hurtful feeling states to injure and separate people from each other.

Research indicates that physical and psychological reactions to not being able to forgive and forget causes blood to clot more quickly, inhibits digestion, and may even be a major contribution to a stroke or heart attack. Creating a new pathway so our minds can deal with ourselves and so that our hearts can deal with others will foster a change in attitude. This will set the forgiver free so that their own wounds will no longer prevent them from forgiving others.

FORGIVENESS STARTS WITH THE SELF

The act of forgiveness is not about condoning evil or ignorant behavior. Instead, it is about first forgiving yourself and then forgiving others for a past action or a debt they can never repay because it is done and too late to do anything about it. If you believe in the ideology that we are on this planet to help each other grow, then it makes sense that there are times when we are either conduits or obstacles to one another. That's why some of our worst experiences turn out to be our most growthful and why our most difficult teachers are often the ones who make the most difference in our lives. The paradoxes of these lessons are humanly difficult and yet spiritually surmountable. Our journey is about learning how to go through the process of forgiving the person, not the actions. This concept can be a powerful turning point in anyone's life.

Consider the example of a divorced couple. Reuniting after a long separation is not an easy task. This "forgiving" experience can be painfully difficult and confusing because of an underlying fear of the past repeating itself, which is precisely the pain that keeps people apart. So how do you heal and open up at the same time? It may not be easy; however, it is doable.

What helps the process most is an understanding of self—defining your own issues, needs, and wants—and also the understanding that we all act out in a way that is reflective of our own conditioning. These patterns alienate us and do not reflect our highest and truest nature. Sir Thomas Brown portrays this when he says, "No man can justly censure or condemn another, because indeed no man truly knows another." The essence of his words clearly supports the truth that we are actually forgiving the person and not the action.

The importance of forgiveness becomes even more apparent when people change, for this is when we are able to see others and ourselves as we truly are. As we individually grow and change, we often see and experience the changing of others. This change reveals itself before our own eyes as the story of life unfolds.

Here's a brilliant quote that shows how change and forgiveness relate: "The stupid neither forgive nor forget; the naive forgive and forget; the wise forgive but do not forget." The

initial anger coupled with not forgetting is important because it is this feeling and act of knowing that enables us to set appropriate boundaries and protect ourselves as we continue to raise our standards, grow, and change. Even after crumbling, relationships continue to grow because new footings have been established that will support it on another plane.

COURAGE IN COMMUNICATION

Being honest with yourself and others about how you feel takes courage. As this courage unfolds from your heart, you become more responsible, accountable, and let go of the need to blame others. As the other person gets a chance to release emotions, we become mindful about what is actually going on. We realize that this moment is about the movie of their life, not ours. We can feel angry, hurt, and disappointed with and for them; however, this understanding enables us to spend our energy becoming more accountable and self-responsible, and not blaming others.

Just as "I" language helps diffuse anger, so too does it aid in communication in general. "I" language prevents us from making assumptions about the other person, because the focus is on what we need to do for ourselves. Here's an example: "When you didn't show up for our dinner engagement, I felt hurt and disappointed because friendships are important to me and I value our friendship. I also felt angry because had I known you weren't coming, I would not have prepared such a special meal and would have made other plans."

The above example illustrates how you are able to get in touch with your feelings, be responsible and accountable as you sort out whose issues belong to whom, express your truths, and refrain from mind reading and blaming by not making any false assumptions or taking things personally. It also further illustrates how you can avoid anger as you understand and develop a sense of boundary that will serve to change the relationship for the better.

No one possesses the power or control to undo something that has been said or done to us because it is part of the

126

past. It is too late to change it or get it back. To hold on to the negative emotions associated with the words or deed keeps us stuck. When we stay attached to the memory of past grievances, our behaviors exhibit negativity. We instead need to move forward and experience forgiveness, faith, trust, love, and compassion. Only then can we change. This experience is empowering and allows us to heal as we forgive. As difficult as it can be at times to open up for fear of possible hurt or pain, the effort is vital to healing. The act of forgiveness is born out of love, and it is a change that takes great courage, compassion, and understanding to accomplish.

THE LANGUAGE OF LOVE

Unconditional love is pure, without demands, expectations, or conditions. It is both patient and kind, and it bears all things, believes all things, hopes all things, and endures all things. Unconditional love is so true that it never ends.

Love can repair damaged relationships, heal wounds, and make us whole as we learn to let go of judgments. It is the first step toward attaining "invulnerability"—a place of truth and honesty where we are truly coming from the heart and where we can be ourselves without wearing masks or becoming defensive.

Compassion is the key that opens the door to this love. Fyodor Dostoyevsky displays a sense of spiritual elegance when he makes his point that "Compassion is the chief law of human existence." We have the opportunity to practice compassion through acts of forgiveness and by releasing resentments, anger, and hurt. Forgiveness represents freedom and peace, which we are so deserving of. It follows awareness and understanding and emanates from the heart. We understand what it means to forgive when we realize that every act can be an expression of love.

Alexander Pope said: "To err is human; to forgive, divine." This profound level of understanding enables us to change our reality and get past the resentment that sometimes creeps up into our lives. Think of it as a growthful opportunity that

opens new doors to greater wisdom. When we forgive, we become energized instead of losing energy and weakening our immune system with negative emotional states. Ultimately, life without love, caring relationships, compassion, wisdom, and forgiveness would indeed be a sour experience.

QUESTIONS TO PONDER:
- ♦ *For what actions or words do I need to forgive myself?*
- ♦ *Who am I harboring resentment towards?*
- ♦ *What is preventing me from forgiving others?*

FOCUS ON THE JOURNEY, NOT THE END RESULT

Life is a journey filled with lessons. Many of us have consciously and unconsciously experienced much along this walk of life. These lessons enable us to understand what it means to go from a state of unconscious incompetent to one of unconscious competent.

When we look at life as a series of lessons, we realize that there are no mistakes. Our failures along the way serve to unravel the mystery of what it is we need to know for the next part of our journey. Thomas Edison learned a small lesson each time he came up with one of the 1,600 failures for inventing the incandescent bulb. A contemporary example would be Michael Jordan when he said, "I have missed more than 9,000 shots in my career. I have lost almost 300 games. On 26 occasions I have been entrusted to take the game winning shot...and I missed. And I have failed over and over and over again in my life. And that is precisely why I succeed." Clearly, each experience is necessary for the next step or level. All in all, we can say that failures are instrumental to our succeeding, as they allow us to take a chance, try something different, and learn what doesn't work.

A dear friend of mine shared a lovely story with me one day. And I in turn would like to take a moment to share it with you.

The Station

by Robert J. Hastings

Tucked away in our subconscious is an idyllic vision. We see ourselves on a long trip that spans the continent. We are traveling by train. Out the windows we drink in the passing scene of cars on nearby highways, of children waving at a crossing, of cattle grazing on a distant hillside, of smoke pouring from a power plant, of row upon row of corn and wheat, of flatlands and valleys, of mountains and rolling hillsides, of city skylines and village halls.

But uppermost in our minds is the final destination. On a certain day at a certain hour we will pull into the station. Bands will be playing and flags waving. Once we get there so many wonderful dreams will come true and the pieces of our lives will fit together like a completed jigsaw puzzle. How restlessly we pace the aisles, damning the minutes for loitering— waiting, waiting, waiting for the station.

"When we reach the station, that will be it!" we cry. "When I'm 18!" "When I buy a new SL Mercedes Benz!" "When I put the last kid through college!" "When I have paid off the mortgage!" "When I get a promotion!" "When I reach the age of retirement, I shall live happily ever after!"

Sooner or later we must realize there is no station, no one place to arrive at once and for all. The true joy of life is the trip. The station is only a dream. It constantly outdistances us.

"Relish the moment" is a good motto, especially when coupled with Psalm 118:24: "This is the day, which the Lord hath made, we will rejoice and be glad in it." It isn't the burdens of today that drive men mad. It is the regrets over yesterday and the fear of tomorrow. Regret and fear are twin thieves who rob us of today.

So stop pacing the aisles and counting the miles. Instead, climb more mountains, eat more ice cream, go barefoot more often, swim more rivers, watch more sunsets, laugh more,

cry less. Life must be lived as we go along. The station will come soon enough.

I share this story with you because I want you to learn to trust yourself as you rely on your intuition. Choices based on intellect alone are not always the best. When you are in the flow, you discover certain truths about yourself; therefore, decisions no longer become necessary. Life becomes a matter of choices, which require much less energy. We create our future with the energy we put into the present. So when we ask ourselves "What is most important today?" and "What is it I need to do today?", we are making the present good. Then the future has a way of taking care of itself. Allow your values to guide the direction you follow and life becomes more effortless. It is about accepting the present as perfect.

This is not to say that ultimate perfection in the present always feels perfect. However, when we look back it seems as though it all turned out just the way it was intended to be. This reminds me of a story about the Greek temple builders. The Greeks felt that there was no such thing as true perfection. Therefore, they built their temples with slight flaws, consciously not making them totally symmetrical. But when we look at their work today, it all seems perfect, doesn't it?

LIFE'S SPIRITUAL JOURNEY

Our experiences in life are indicative of our spiritual path—the road that takes us on our journey. The interplay that exists between awareness, action, and growth continually evolves and moves us toward accepting the connectivity between all things and recognizing its ultimate perfection. Here's how this happens: Consider a belief system that supports the ideology of the spiritual principles and language in this book. Add to that individual laws and beliefs that constitute ideas to help us understand and experience spiritual connections as we journey on our path. These levels of awareness are progressions of growth that can either be suggested or intuitive.

For example, let's consider the game of life and the rules by which we play. If I believe that my rules for life have to do with being as competitive as I can be and that I am attached to the idea of having to win at all costs, then obviously there will always be a winner and a loser in all I do. With this dynamic, the loser experiences feelings of fear, disappointment, frustration, failure, rejection, blaming, and eventually experiences a "slow spiritual death." However, if I enter into the game of life with a set of rules that enables me to be and do my best without having an attachment to winning at all costs, then I am actually playing from a "centered position." This place is so focused on being and doing that there is no time to contemplate fear, failure, rejection, blaming, or the eventual slow spiritual death.

Now let's take this individual situation and apply it to a relationship so we can see how each person projects and reflects their experience. Suppose there are two people who are committed to making a relationship work. I'll contrast the experience to that of climbing what seems to be an insurmountable mountain. Partner one wants the relationship to work and climbs the mountain with the intended outcome that this relationship will be what is it meant to be without having an attachment to the intended result. Partner two is also committed to the relationship and is determined to do whatever it takes to make the relationship work and bring it to new heights; partner two is attached to the outcome. Reaching the intended pinnacle of having two people aligned with each other and in a healthy relationship is the ultimate dream for both.

Along this long and arduous journey, the relationship sours and partner two begins feeling disappointment, depression, and frustration that the two people are not ultimately suited for one another. Partner one also feels disappointed and sad that the relationship is not working but doesn't experience the negative emotions that partner two does. In fact, partner one comes to the conclusion that although he or she wanted the relationship, it was not the right relationship for either of them.

Why the difference in feelings? Partner one's individual sense of success was focused on a stronger sense of self in terms

of both individual and relationship wants and needs. On the other hand, partner two, who was so determined to make the relationship work, was painfully attached to the outcome. Partner two experienced an overwhelming sense of failure, believing that he or she never reached the top of the mountain because the end result was one of union with the other instead of union with oneself first.

Accepting what is for our own growth and focusing energy toward making it as perfect as it possibly can be may not always be the easiest choice, especially when it comes to matters of the heart; however, it is often the wisest. Enjoying the present is to experience a state of "relaxed attentiveness" that leaves no room for judgment or preoccupations with the past or future.

The Journey Continues

Focusing on the journey and not the destination enables us to live in the present more fully and experience who we are and what we want to be. For example, as we live in the present and experience emotions or sensations, these feelings are linked to past or present thoughts. When we experience pain in the present, it represents hurt. If that hurt represents a thought from the past, then perhaps the pain manifests itself as anger, or if it is linked to a thought in the future, then perhaps as anxiety. This is why it is so important to take responsibility for yourself, deal with the issues of the past, put them away, and live in the present. This takes both practice and willingness to develop the skills for purposeful living.

To put it more concretely, experts have estimated that the average person has 60,000 thoughts per day. Of those, 75 percent have to do with past or future experiences rather than present ones. What compounds this estimate is that approximately 90 percent of those thoughts are repetitious. Now you can understand how wasteful it is to allow yesterday's business to eat away at today.

Living in the moment (in the present) is an alien strategy to the physical realities of our world because it requires us to live in ambiguity. Our society does not promote this type of conscious living. "Not knowing is invalidated;" therefore it is not okay to live our lives without knowing what is next. This is part of the reason for going through the purification ritual that will allow you to be your true self.

Focusing on the present means being fully aware and giving your full attention to what is going on now at this moment. Then, when the moment is passed, you can let it go. Thich Nhat Hanh, a prominent Vietnamese Buddhist monk/teacher, says, "People have a hard time letting go of their suffering. Out of a fear of the unknown, they prefer suffering that is familiar."

This is why "mindful living" is so important. It enables you to monitor your thoughts without judgment and become the observer. You can literally step outside of yourself. Being the observer allows you to live in the present without the baggage of the past or the anxiety of the future. It is a powerful method of "letting go" and coming from your highest self.

QUESTIONS TO PONDER:
- *How much time do I spend living in the past or future?*
- *What is keeping me from living in the present?*
- *What are the lessons I am learning on my journey that enable me to be fully present?*

HAPPINESS IS NOT WHAT YOU WANT, BUT WHAT YOU GET
Have you ever experienced situations in your life where you wanted something, didn't get it, and felt awful? Do you still harbor those "awful" feelings many years later when you think back to the situation? Image how you would feel if you adopted the following beliefs instead.

- Everything happens in the perfect time and space sequence, and I release the struggle of trying to make things happen.
- All is well in my world, and I trust the Universe to take me where it is I need to go. Wherever that is will be for my highest good and the common good of all.

- Situations are neither good nor bad. They just "are." I have the inner wisdom and common sense to be responsible, accept the situation, and be positive.

These types of beliefs help us put things in a different perspective so that we can handle the ongoing life situations involving family, friends, homes, jobs, and love. Unfortunately, some people never understand that happiness is not always what we wanted or expected.

Happiness is not an external condition, but rather a conscious decision to accept the normal conflicts of life as part of everyday living. This is a daunting challenge because life is a collection of experiences, and again there is a continual interchange between human will and Divine Providence. This forces us to come face-to-face with another life paradox: The "language of love" and the "language of the Gods" come from the same place, and when we follow the path to that place, we can easily get sidetracked with the "language of the physical world" in which we live.

I shy away from using this term loosely because it is the world with rules and regulations that we have become accustomed to and enslaved by. In the words of Edgar Cayce, "We are not physical beings having a spiritual experience. We are spiritual beings having a physical experience." For the most part, the physical world in which we live easily communicates misguided dreams. Happiness becomes the acquisition of things or possessions. In reality, happiness in not necessarily the home, the spouse, the car, etc.; happiness is within us. It is about "soul," and what enriches the soul is the act of giving instead of acquiring. Giving fosters a place of freedom and an everlasting sense of prosperity, while acquiring involves feeling owned and burdened.

We have a choice as to whether we want to live as consumers or givers. This is not to discount the fact that human beings do enjoy acquiring things. However, it is important to employ self-questioning tactics on what the specific motives for acquisition are. During those moments of feeling "boxed in," ask yourself, "What is the lesson or teaching I need to learn from this experience? Is it endurance, patience, courage, or whatever else may sound true?"

THE HAPPINESS PARADOX

Sometimes we experience feelings of exasperation from repeatedly trying to achieve and accomplish things to no avail. The blocked expression often sounds like this: "No matter what I try nothing seems to happen." Consider looking at the situation in a different way. Even though we may feel we are ready to move on, perhaps the Universe has other plans at the moment. It is in these darkest moments that gratitude is so important, because if it were not for these times, then the opportunity to experience a greater richness in life would not exist.

There is a reason for everything that happens, and it has nothing to do with right or wrong, good or bad. Rather than retreat into feelings of self-doubt, be thankful for what is, ask for the grace to accept it, and continue to have faith, trust, and love. This state of acceptance welcomes us to a place of openness that embraces trust to go forward without attachment. Clearly, this demands courage. Metaphorically, fairy tales notoriously talk about going to the Wizard for "courage;" it's no different than real life situations of going to our Higher Power.

Whatever evolves will be for a good reason. However, if you're living in the past or future, you can get distracted and hang on to the way you want things or the way you feel they should be. Happiness usually ends up to be what you get, and that is usually the best surprise of all. I'm convinced that when a lot of small stuff goes wrong, that only means something very beautiful is going to happen.

I remember a realtor friend who desperately wanted to relocate to a nearby condo community that would meet her every need. However, she couldn't sell her current home. As she watched each available condo unit sell one by one, her frustration continued to mount. Being a real estate agent herself, she tried every conceivable strategy to sell her home, but nothing

worked. After many months of this, her negative feelings began to overwhelm her.

When she finally decided to let the idea go and stay at her current residence, the builder called her with an opportunity to purchase "the last available unit," and he offered her incredible terms to make it happen. I remember her saying that she pinched herself to make sure she was awake and not dreaming the whole conversation. And guess what, two weeks later her current home sold!

Looking back, her situation certainly encompassed stress regarding financial issues, the selling of a home, and the purchase of another one. However, after all was said and done, she knew that in the end it was all perfect. It truly was happiness, but nothing like she had ever imagined.

Very often, the gratitude and appreciation that follows life's situations are beyond words. For many of us, wealth is living each day with an attitude of gratitude. As we build our gardens of gratitude, it becomes increasingly more important to plant these seeds, water them, and watch them grow. As we engage in this process and develop a heightened sense of awareness, we become more mindful and capable of dealing with some of the weeds that may have a tendency to grow, such as negativity, fear, hesitancy, and indecision. Planting, watering, and weeding are all part of the process of achieving beauty and potential.

Allow gratitude to always be present and overwhelming, even during difficult times. Being thankful for the most challenging times in life comes with knowing that obstacles exist to encourage personal growth. Appreciate the people who come and go in your life. Using these moments helps us learn how to develop a sense of balance and be respectful of the diversity of others.

I often hear people say how others are not grateful at times. Because one person does a good deed for another, there sometimes seems to be an expectation of wanting a thank you or acknowledgement in return. The remedy lies in asking yourself, "Am I doing this for another and myself? Or, am I doing this for another and myself with the expectation that people *should* express gratitude?" Your answer determines your outlook.

DISCOVER THE JOY OF GIVING WITHOUT EXPECTATION

When I was a child, my great aunt used to say, "When you do a good deed it is not necessary to let the right hand know what the left hand is doing. Then it is a genuine, true gift from the heart that needs no glorification." Giving without expectation denotes a strong foundation that resonates with confidence and wholeness instead of neediness. When deeds are focused around expectation, there is a desire for reciprocation. When that desire gets misconstrued as a "must need," the ego feels insecure and unrest prevails.

Happiness understands and accepts the fact that gratitude is a cultivated trait. When Jesus healed 10 lepers, only one returned to thank him. It is similar to planting seeds in a garden. As we cultivate an attitude of gratitude and learn to use it, it grows. We only need to remember to water the seeds regularly and let them grow.

One year over a Thanksgiving holiday, our family discussed the idea of what it would be like to plant a garden. Some of us talked about never having done that while others responded with what a good feeling gardening gave them. We then discussed what it would be like if we planted a garden of gratitude. It was a fun exercise with everyone revealing things they were grateful for. At first the responses were tight, then they loosened up a bit, and before we knew it, we were speaking for each other. Smiles, joyous laughter, gratefulness, and stories ensued. This type of garden grows from daily thoughts and creates a shift in the way we think, feel, and act.

INTUITIVE HAPPINESS

What does intuition have to do with happiness? To understand the connection, it is important to recognize intuition as a gift or an insight that whispers the truth. It can be a feeling or a sense that someone is watching or standing behind you, a rapid pulse

rate, a queasy feeling in the pit of your stomach, or even a burst of inspiration. Intuition doesn't argue, threaten, or have a loud, demanding voice; rather, it is a soft gentle voice that supports and stretches you. Often times it poses choices that require courage, patience, and faith. There is no right or wrong in this place. The idea is to welcome it, trust it, give it full attention, and be grateful for it.

Instinct is that voice that says "I don't think so" or "Why not; go for it; what are you waiting for?" Whenever I have not trusted my intuition, I have paid the price. Many people ignore their instinct for fear of the unknown. They are unsure of where following their instinct will take them, so they choose to disregard it. However, not knowing is often a good thing. When you seek the newness of an experience, you can create it and feel the sense of adventure, fun, excitement, happiness, and enthusiasm of the moment. You put your fears behind you and just trust. I have often felt that not knowing is actually safer than knowing, since there is no concrete situation that may cause you to worry about the things that did not work or the intimidation of what the future may hold. It is a place of being in the present and moving forward.

As we begin to utilize and incorporate raised standards, beliefs, and strategies into our lives, we automatically exude a sense of inner happiness. The next step necessary to close the loop and create outer happiness is to develop and share our gifts with others. Becoming aware of these gifts and talents and learning to use them wisely gives us another golden opportunity to practice gratitude as we take the time to genuinely appreciate and honor ourselves. The more we exercise this principle the more we grow, and so here in lies our treasure—the treasure of wealth that supports happiness and well-being.

This wellspring of wealth can also provide a platform for becoming more effective. We can manage our time more wisely, whether it be by delegating more, investing in automation, or just managing day-to-day activities in an efficient manner.

Consider the following tips:

- Invest 10 percent of your time in yourself, whether it be in education, training, or self-development.
- Put aside one day a week to nurture yourself. After all, you are your greatest tangible asset.
- Develop a sense of well-being without feeling overwhelmed. Continue to work toward simplifying your life. For example, if one of your goals is to create financial independence, then create a plan that would simply your life with a budget. Did you know that in some households 10 to 20 percent of its income could be attributed to negative expenses that are superfluous and contribute to trying to "make oneself feel good?" Perhaps there is nothing wrong with that when you are not trying to simplify your life with a budget; however, when these needs are met, people are less likely to spend needlessly and do experience an opportunity to eliminate unnecessary expenses without significant reductions in profitability, quality, and happiness.
- Consider a plan to cut expenses, save more each day, and invest in a fund that would double your income within a specific number of years. Be mindful of the fact that it is important to identify the lifestyle you want to achieve. For example, if your income is $5,000 per month, then live on a budget that would leave 5 to 10 percent of your income for savings after taxes. When lifestyle begins to dominate, it takes a form of ownership that makes it difficult to maintain integrity. If freedom and integrity are more important than lifestyle, then find ways in which to cut expenses in order to have a simplified, sustainable life. If lifestyle is more important, then find ways to increase the income.

QUESTIONS TO PONDER:
- *What does happiness mean to me?*
- *What are the things that make me happy and grateful?*
- *Do I trust my intuition to move me forward? If not, what's holding me back?*

♦ *How can I utilize my sense of inner and outer happiness to grow and create a life of gratitude that gives me peace of mind, body, and spirit?*

SURRENDER VS. RESISTANCE

To "surrender" is a behavior change. Giving up power and making peace with "another force or forces" is an apt description of the term. Surrender follows acceptance, meaning that once you have accepted something, the inclination to fight, deny or resist dissipates. You become empowered to act differently and go one step further to actively include a new truth in your life.

Resistance is the opposite of surrender and is linked to fear. It can be referred to as a form of "protection." Of all the fears known, rejection and abandonment, which are both rooted in isolation, are the greatest. What's interesting is that all fear is our own making. When we think of fear as "**F**alse **E**vidence or **E**xpectations that **A**ppear **R**eal," we see that our fear stems from our perceptions of anticipated events. Fear gets its power from the future. The best way to circumvent the "what ifs" is to be in the present, knowing that we only have this moment, and that this moment is safe.

Use fear as a source of strength, because when you do the things you fear, the death of that fear is certain. Create beliefs that are larger than your fears and allow yourself to feel "empowered." In addition, consider this exquisite proverb from 2 Timothy 1:7 that speaks loud to this emotion: "For God has not given us the spirit of fear, but of power, and of love, and of sound mind."

GETTING TO THE HEART OF FEAR

Let me share with you a story that reflects one man's incredible strength and courage to abandon the human conditioning that created barriers of fear and resistance. "Joe" was an intelligent, charming, charismatic, and successful man who had an insatiable inner drive. His constant quest for accomplishment made it difficult for him to achieve a sense of inner peace and fulfillment in his life. He knew his life was out of balance, yet he did not understand the reasons why.

Additionally, Joe had an inability to share intimate relationships. Often when I tried to engage in a conversation with him, the situation was difficult. His highly competitive nature made his communication style one of challenge and counterchallenge. His confrontational approach turned each conversation into a debate. In his mind, there always had to be a winner and a loser.

One day I suggested that Joe get psychological help. He agreed, and simultaneously we continued to move forward with a plan heavily focused on defining needs, identifying beliefs, and instilling better communication skills. This was a lengthy process, because it involved having him get in touch with his true self—his heart. In order for this to work, he needed the reassurance that he was in a safe place.

During the course of our working together, I observed that Joe would often talk about his childhood. One day, Joe related a story to me that was rather chilling, yet it made me understand where he was coming from.

When Joe was a boy, his father put boxing gloves on him and took him around the block to find other children to fight with. Being a child, Joe found this experience quite painful; however, he believed that his father loved him and he wanted to please him, so he masked the pain and mustered the courage and strength to fight the bullies. Over time, Joe became conditioned to believing this was a principle law of "survival." His perceived world dictated a different set of rules, whereby people need to defend themselves at all costs while burying the notion of trust.

Survival became a competition for Joe, as he spent much of his life defending himself against others. It was always a measure of who was bigger and better—who was the winner and who was the loser. By continually defending himself, Joe was draining his energy and losing himself and all the feelings that went with that true self. It was no wonder that Joe turned out the way he was—conditioned to believing that it is not safe

to express your feelings or come from your heart where you can be open and trusting. Joe's world was not a safe place; therefore, trust and the ability to feel did not exist.

This leads to both a question and an understanding of "How could Joe avoid sabotaging himself when he was not able to experience healthy relationships because he wore the mask of 'having to be strong without showing vulnerability.'" The paradox of it all is that vulnerability is a manifestation of the externally driven ego, while invulnerability is a manifestation of the internally driven true self.

In order for Joe to come from his heart, he would need to put his ego on the shelf. His ego, created out of childhood survival, was based on guilt and insecurity. It is this form of "life protection" that required a continual sense of power and the need to control and preserve that power. For Joe, the fear of losing and rejection was greater than who he thought he was.

When a person's self concept struggles with fear, it is often the fear that wins. No wonder Joe was not at peace. He could not be his true self because he was constantly at war within himself. His ego, which was based in a "should or right way," fashioned denial, defensiveness, selfishness, a closed and stuck feeling, dishonesty, a false self image, and fear. These traits are certainly not congruent with the natural part of the true self coming from love. A self that is based in "your way," manifests truth, honesty, awareness, defenselessness, selflessness, and safety.

Joe learned his behavioral patterns from his role model. His conditioned behaviors were rituals—habitual ways of seeing the world. This is part of the reason for Joe's imbalance. His unconscious incompetent behavior patterns prevented personal growth and required inordinate amounts of energy to keep his fear intact.

Since Joe was getting appropriate therapy, we were able to effectively work together toward helping him understand his behavioral patterns and identify the coping barriers he had created. With this newfound knowledge, Joe began to take a more relaxed approach to life, and enjoy richer, more rewarding relationships. At last he found inner peace. For him, this knowledge represented happiness and success.

THE THREE C'S OF SURRENDER

As you experience the transition of going from resistance to surrender, you will find yourself experiencing less pain and discomfort. The feeling is like going from belief to faith. At some point the switch to faith comes into play because the events or outcome are no longer tangible. The feeling of being stuck, where energy is connected to pain, creates a sense of "numbness."

Surrendering comes from a place of truth and love. After surrender, a feeling of commitment and trust evolves along with our initial acceptance. Just as we had previously planted a garden of gratitude, we can now add surrender to that flowerbed, knowing that the more we nurture these seeds, the more we will flourish. It is a place of integration with the mind, body, and spirit.

As you come to terms with the concept of surrender, it's important to build up reserves of love. The ability to relate well to yourself and others and experience love is an important component of any human being. To help put your relationships with yourself and others in perspective, and to foster an acceptance of surrender, follow the three C's of Control, Causation, and Creation. These are useful strategic tools that help secure a place of understanding, acceptance, and restoration within yourself. The technique requires you to ask yourself the following questions:

- Do I have control over this person or situation?
- Did I cause this person or situation?
- Did I create this person or situation?

If the above three questions elicited a "no" response from you, then relax; you're on the right track. These questions allow you to artfully put things in perspective and relate to what you are and are not responsible for so you can become more centered and move on.

143

QUESTIONS TO PONDER:
- *Am I feeling resistance in my life and in what areas?*
- *What is it I have to do to surrender?*
- *What is keeping me from surrendering?*

RELEASE ATTACHMENTS AND EXPECTATIONS

Very often, our expectations cause our problems. When we release our expectations and attachments, we feel "in the flow" of life. This realization represents the alignment of self with energy that already exists. It brings you to a place where natural strengths lie—a place where there is surrender, truth, and love.

Releasing attachments and expectations is not about "things;" it is about the energy and spiritual philosophy we attach to those things that impede our progress toward being free to respond appropriately. At that point, the "musts" and "shoulds" dissolve. Taking in acceptance in terms of expanding your experiences of the world helps you bask in the rays of gratitude, love, and truth.

A LESSON OF FAITH

Whenever I hear the expression "making lemonade out of lemons," I smile because I have come to realize that even lemons are useful. The lessons we learn as a result of our "lemon" experiences certainly add credence and strength to our growth and development. For example, I remember a time when I was quite ill. I had contracted Lyme's disease and was suffering with the late stages of it after a three-year period. The joint pain, headaches, neurological damage, and moments of impaired memory were more than I could bear at times.

There were also many other demands going on in my life at the time. In addition to being a mother, wife, and full-time student in my last semester of college, there was also a household to manage, a family to take care of, as well as home renovations—all going on at the same time. And of course, there was the medical treatment.

Rather than be hospitalized, I chose to be an outpatient at the hospital for my daily intravenous treatment. It clearly was a trying period, and at times I wondered how I would ever get through it all. Feeling the intense pain, along with moments of tears and despair, coupled with the anxiety of wondering what the future would hold for me was a challenge indeed. *Would I get getter? Could I get better?* One thing was for sure was the faith, love, and support of family and friends. The power of prayer to this day will always be with me along with those who prayed so hard. There is no question in my mind that it was this phenomenal source of faith, trust, and love that gave me the strength to persevere, recover and be grateful.

Throughout it all, I knew in my heart that my energy would be much better spent if I focused on what I had to do to get well rather than on worrying. Learning the importance of the "power of faith" and "mindful living" paved a new pathway for me. It prompted me to notice that the people coming into my life were a "gift" and not a mistake. In many instances, I truly felt as though they were my guardians. They were there for a purpose, and it was to help me through this bleak period in my life.

The power of my prayer and faith was a clear representation of a Higher Source that rested within and around me. My beliefs needed to be strong, and I needed to continue to secure my faith as I worked on attitude, perseverance, persistence, and tenacity. Realizing that my attitude comprised 90 percent of my reactions to things and that persistence was a known measure of my courage and faith enabled me to use these qualities to my advantage. I became conscious of the elements I had no control of, and coming to terms with them was yet another growthful experience. I discovered a power within me to persevere and do what was necessary to heal. My doctor smiled when I said that my job was to get better while his job was to figure out what he had to do to make it happen. What a relief! At that point it was useless for me to expend any energy on worrying about his task because I understood what I had to do for myself.

VENTURING INTO UNCHARTERED WATERS

All of us experience the protection of Divine Intervention in our lives. Surrendering without attachments or expectations and trusting that the rest is up to God enabled me to swim with grace in "unchartered waters." As I reflect on my past illness and other life events, I realize that "I am safe, my life and actions are divinely guided, and I live and grow in peace, security, and serenity every moment of my life." I have been fortunate to experience the healing effects of these learned spiritual beliefs that have provided me with an incredible source of strength. Although this journey can include feeling insecure and out of control at times, it is these very elements that lead us to a new dimension of ourselves.

When dealing with certain situations in life that you have control over, consider yourself in "chartered" waters. Here is where you can use all the facts and logic to your advantage. However, when you are in situations you have no control over, such as dealing with a life-threatening illness or some other catastrophic event, you find yourself in "unchartered" waters. While encountering this course of events, no amount of facts or logic will suffice. In a broad sense, here is where the concept of faith enters and dares the soul to go beyond what the eyes can see. In these situations, we are dealing with issues of fear, and the only known cure is faith. This belief enables us to "accept," and this acceptance changes our attitude.

When your expectations are not met and you don't get what you want, you acquire an "experience." Part of the experience is giving up resistance and agreeing to a prevailing set of circumstances without attachments. In so doing, you come full circle with a behavior change, because you have surrendered without having expectations or attachments to the outcome. When this occurs, a new truth or action enters your life. Metaphorically, an awareness and a shift are simultaneously occurring. As your awareness of information and clarity blends with your shift of taking action, the opportunity to "walk your talk" becomes unequalled, representing a profound breakthrough experience.

As you traverse through unchartered waters, you may feel as though you have lost your way. This is when it is useful to tune into your internal language of acceptance, for it will take you the rest of the way. It's a matter of going from a concrete *belief* that says, "Yes, this will be fine; the evidence of this outcome is apparent," to a place of faith where there is no such tangible evidence to support that belief. Emerging changed with no perceptions of what that change will be is both humbling and growthful. When you turn to faith, there is a non-materialistic spiritual concept that manifests itself in wholeness. It is an energetic shift from hoping to thinking to believing to listening to living. The Bible defines it as "the substance of things hoped for, the evidence of things not seen." Hebrews 11:1.

Hope becomes the fertile ground upon which the seeds of faith grow and energize a new way of thinking, believing, and living. Thus, faith allows us the freedom to know that no matter what happens, we are one with our Higher Force and that the needed wisdom, strength, and courage will be close at hand. When we embrace the mystery of faith into our lives, we allow ourselves the wonder of being alive.

Faith is a gift that tells us when to surrender versus when to resist. The miracle of faith understands the spiritual principle that our journeys are about what "life expects of us versus what we expect of it," and the best-known strategy I know is "letting go and letting God." I suspect Joseph Campbell resonated the same message when he said, "We must be willing to get rid of the life we've planned, so as to have the life that is waiting for us."

QUESTIONS TO PONDER:
- *What are my limiting beliefs, expectations, and attitudes?*
- *What happens when I detach from those expectations?*
- *What is it I have to do to detach from them?*
- *How can I use my faith in the process?*

THE GIFT OF SPIRITUALITY

Spirituality is what gives life credence and direction. It is the wellspring from which all life comes and is clearly about beliefs, what we do with those beliefs, and how committed we are to making them happen. Being aware of what we need to know and simultaneously taking the necessary action is what creates a strong and sustainable foundation. This sense of Spirit gives sacredness to a mundane life.

Having the belief of "I can" coupled with the intentionality of what "I want" to do and feeling determined that "I'm going to do it" is a powerful combination. It is this sense of willful commitment that says "I have to" and that pulls it all together and makes it work. This presence rests close to a person and brings healing.

Spirituality is a profound part of us that is unique by design. When we embrace our spirituality, we see its elegance and learn ways to use it for our higher good and the common good of all. When we are in tune to our spiritual side, we can meet life's challenges with open hearts and minds, while having a sense of security knowing that in the end all is well.

The following prayer, called *True Prayer*, is a spiritual gift because it encapsulates and reflects the beauty of the paradoxes that exist between the language of spirituality and our humanity. Take a moment to reflect how the words and meaning of this prayer show life in a different perspective as it presents the path that will show us the perfect way.

An unknown author penned these words:

True Prayer

I asked God to take away my pride. God said, "No. It is not for me to take away, but for you to give it up."

I asked God to make my handicapped child whole. God said, "No. Her spirit is whole, her body is only temporary."

I asked God to grant me patience. God said, "No.
Patience is a by-product of tribulations; it isn't granted;
it is earned.

I asked God to grant me happiness. God said, "No.
I give you blessings; happiness is up to you."

I asked God to spare me pain. God said, "No.
Suffering draws you apart from worldly
cares and brings you closer to me."

I asked God to make my spirit grow. God said,
"No. You must grow on your own, but I will
prune you to make you fruitful."

I asked for all things that I might enjoy life. God
said, "No. I will give you life so that you may
enjoy all things."

I asked God to help me love others as much as
God loves me. God said, "Ahhhh, finally you
have the idea!"

Someone once said that maturity in prayer occurs when
we are able to move from the plea, "give me" to the deeper
prayer, "Use me."

QUESTIONS TO PONDER:
♦ *How can I evoke my Spirituality to give Sacredness to my
 life?*
♦ *What are my beliefs, expectations, and attitudes that reflect a human perspective?*
♦ *What are my beliefs, expectations, and attitudes that reflect a spiritual perspective?*
♦ *How can I use my spiritual belief system to heighten my
 humanity?*

PLATINUM VS. GOLDEN RULE

Many people want to meet that special someone and will go to great lengths to do so. Ironically, many of these people have already met that "special someone," but they have not yet discovered it for themselves.

Couples often share similar interests, likes, and dislikes. However, when one person feels unloved because they are not receiving loving messages in a way that suits their communication style, tension and conflict result. We need to communicate our needs on how we want our partners to love us so they will understand and recognize the appropriate strategy that works. What we usually experience are partners showing their love for one another in a way that is congruent with themselves, not the other person.

We all have different strategies for making relationships work. Some people are more inclined to be kinesthetic, while others have a proclivity toward being auditory or visual. Therefore, it becomes clear why there are people who enjoy touching and others who enjoy hearing someone say how much they are loved and appreciated. Still others cherish a dining experience, sports, or visiting museums and theaters as statements of love. Instead of practicing the "Golden Rule," "Do unto others as you would want done unto yourself," I suggest following the "Platinum Rule," "Do unto other as they would want done unto them." The ability to ask, listen, and understand can be a powerful and sustainable approach. Learning to step outside of yourself and experiencing the territory works miracles for our individual selves and for the relationship.

When people neglect to use appropriate communication strategies in their relationships, they display an attitude of stress and tension. What follows is an expectation of "I want and deserve to be loved, and you must love me the way I want to be loved." This expectation originates from a belief that says, "If you loved me then you would touch me or my life in a certain way."

These limiting rules and generalizations mirror our own incongruities and paint us in a box. Therefore, it is necessary to define needs, wants, values, desired outcomes, goals, and set boundaries. As we expand further on the Platinum Rule, consider the following questions and listen carefully to your responses.

- How would I like others to be when they are with me?
- If I could create the perfect parent, significant other, or partner, what would that person be like?
- How am I feeling in this place or with this person?
- Where is my energy level? (Do I feel energized or depleted?)

Once you have thought about the answers to these questions, share them with others and feel the difference of coming from your heart and mind together.

Now continue with the following:

- What have I learned from this situation or experience?
- How is this similar to other experiences I have had?
- What are the resources I need to draw upon to make this situation better?
- How can I utilize these resources so I can bring out the best in me and in others?

As we become the change we want to see in the world, the prevailing thought of self-fulfillment stands before us. This concept of integrating all the parts of ourselves—Mind/Body/Spirit—is a transformational process that we can only achieve through spirituality.

EXPERIENCE YOUR INHERENT GIFTS

One day I was visiting the Roerich Museum and had the most powerful experience. Roerich was a Russian who lived during Russia's great Silver Age, a time of fervent interest in mysticism that came to an end with the horrors of World War I and the 1917 Revolution. As a youth, Roerich studied law, history, philology, and became passionate about art and archaeology. He was a prolific painter, set and costume designer, writer, and was nominated for the Nobel Peace Prize for "raising the cultural levels of nations and the constant promotion of brother-

hood." Part of his passion stemmed from his belief that mankind's progress toward spiritual consciousness is rooted in artistic expression.

Not having known any of this before my visit, I entered the museum and immediately felt a sense of light that penetrated my very being. Paintings from his travels stirred my soul, creating a sense of peace, joy, beauty, and harmony. There was no question that his artistic expression paved the way toward a greater sense of spiritual awareness.

Spirituality that illuminates a belief beyond the self manifests your truest being—one that goes through the purification ritual to be "who you are" instead of "who you are not." This belief in a higher force or energy shines the light toward "Going Home"—a place where there is unlimited potential. Often, the realization of our own great potential is what ultimately frightens us.

Each and every individual is unique. This inherent universal language or bond that lies within serves as a true connection to others. We need only to find it within ourselves in order for us to come alive and begin to discover it in others. We often hear it referred to as "being in the flow" or "in the zone." One day I was attending a service, and during the homily, the minister spoke of a magnificent prayer that talked about our greatness. He then connected many hearts and minds as he shared these beautiful words: "Please God, let me see the good in me no matter how good it is."

Take a moment to reflect on those words and realize the good in you no matter how good it is. Remember, your talents may be few, but your gifts are many. Be mindful of what your inner gifts are as well as those blessed gifts of love, peace, joy, and friendship that have been bestowed upon you.

AWARENESS LEADS TO GREATNESS

The process of going from understanding to integration requires developing a sense of personal awareness geared toward enlightening and empowering the self. It is a process of "evolution toward consciousness." As we face our fears, we grow our souls.

To do this, we need to exercise physical, emotional, mental, and spiritual disciplines to quiet the mind.

For example, when I talk about physical, I mean moving away from food, alcohol, and drug addictions. Emotional is releasing emotions the weak ego creates and learning to observe and act accordingly. Mental is the ability to go from the intellect to a feeling mode. It is the journey from fear to love, ego to heart, without letting the intellect dominate.

Sometimes when we feel confused, our ego is chattering away. This is a manifestation of our intellect being unsettled, and it requires us to ask fewer questions and drop into our feeling mode. Spiritual is accepting that we are the Chosen Ones. We are no mistake, and through the daily practice of meditation and prayer we can become one with the Peace within ourselves.

When we live by our conditioned rules, we set up personal prisons, and yet when we adhere to certain positive disciplines, we quiet our minds and raise our standards. The end result culminates in the development of a personal heart, mind, spirit, and will. Transformation through spirituality is the key to transcendence. We discover a place where there is no separateness and where you are more Spirit and less personality. It's a place where there are no fears or ego domination, and where you can comfortably observe without attachment. You can experience a oneness between the two worlds we live in—energetic and physical.

SUMMATION OF CREATIVE STRATEGIES FOR SPIRITUAL TRANSFORMATION

The flow of energy has its own set of dynamics that can either work for or against us every day. The premise of what I am articulating is that we are pure energy. Our beliefs are our thoughts. Our senses perceive, we process, and our minds interpret. We are connected both consciously and unconsciously to each other, our environment, and ourselves.

Relationships also represent energy, and they are our driving force. So in order to be true to ourselves, we sometimes

need to risk relationships by dealing with issues instead of denying them, whether it be for the sake of peace, safety, or some other reason. Why is this so? Often times we need to give up relationships the way they are in order for them to become something better. Relationships are vital, and we need them to grow. They are a necessary part of our evolution. The inner dialogues we experience affect our relationships. When these dialogues are "weak" ego based, the relationship is slow and fearful. When the dialogues are Spirit based, the relationship is fast, powerful, and full of love. Relationships cannot survive if we go into them thinking about what we can get. They are about giving. Observing and aligning yourself is critical to the process.

SPIRITUAL RELATIONSHIP STRATEGIES

The following process works for many people to help them uncover the root of a relationship challenge. I suggest you give it a try. First, understand that when a situation upsets or frustrates us, we are not necessarily reacting to the situation or person itself, but to our feelings about that particular event. To restore balance, it is important to get in touch with those feelings and understand and accept the fact that the other person is doing his or her best. This principle embodies a level of consciousness that requires us to look deep within ourselves.

The next step is to get in touch with the mask you are wearing. For example, if your significant other spilled a glass of milk and you get angry, you may be asking for perfection. You need to get in touch with that part of yourself that requires perfection because it is a learned part of yourself that may not reflect your true self. The need for perfection may be a conditioned part of yourself that you have adopted because you want to feel loved. Now is when focusing is important.

Observe and experience your breath as a way of bringing yourself back to center. Instead of denying these parts of yourself, attend to them, give them the attention they deserve, and minimize their presence through self-awareness and self-responsibility. You can then exercise your ability to transform yourself by creating a connection with the Breath, Spirit, God,

Universe, or other Higher Power and letting it go.

After going through this process, it is time to define what the issues are and to whom they belong. Then you can define the needed resources (knowledge, understanding, communications skills, etc.) and restore yourself so you can be more in alignment with who you are. Finally, the task is to utilize the necessary resources and calmly communicate your feeling with the "other" in such a way that heals and restores balance.

For example, "When you spilled that glass of milk, I got very upset because it made a mess of things. Messes upset me because I want things to be perfect. But I'm discovering that the world is not perfect. I apologize for over reacting." The "amazing grace" from this experience is that you and the other person change, grow, and are open to new ideas, new insights, and new ways of being so you can both become more of who you are and less of who you're not.

This process enables you to empower yourself and others who are ready and willing to move forward. You can then create "magic" in all your relationships. I define "relationship magic" as a feeling of "authenticity without a mask." It's a peaceful love that calls us to be daring, and a knowing love that is a choice in the highest form of living—a never failing love.

THE POWER OF INTENTION

When we want to attract a particular person or thing in our lives, being mindful of "intention" and aligning ourselves with our values and our essence is vital. Knowing what you want and expressing it verbally allows you to enfold knowledge and intention together. Doing this enables you to frame your intention and put it out there in a world of energy called the "field of awareness."

A friend of mine who had been divorced for a number of years wanted to find a suitable mate whom she could marry and share the rest of her life with. She followed this exercise and put her intention out with all the particulars—age, height, mannerisms, hobbies, interests, etc. She eventually attracted the man

of her dreams; however, there was one small problem—he was married. Being specific and thorough with your intention is obviously necessary. All in all it was an interesting lesson, one that enabled her to know how to be more specific and attract an even more suitable *unmarried* partner.

As you frame your real intention, believe in it and trust with an open spirit that the Universe will respond. Release the things that undermine it, such as worry, fear, or uncertainty. Equally important is to let go of the "weak" ego mind—your desires, attachments, and judgments. Surrender to the synchronicity that unfolds and pay attention to the feedback, allowing the Universe to work for you. Feel the pull sensation versus the push effort and refrain from controlling situations that are beyond your control. Pay attention to the emotional turbulence along the way and use those experiences to seek the messages, teachings, and lessons given and received. Allow yourself to continually seek that peace of self, your highest truth, the authenticity that enables you to be your brilliant and creative self as you journey through life continually learning, growing, and evolving towards your highest potential.

You have the ability to use your creativity to create your self, to find your soul as you embrace your shadow, and to heal through reconciliation and forgiveness. Once again, this sense of creativity enables you to *find your soul so that it can perform its job to wake up the self, to experience your true being as you become more of your authentic self, and to exercise your passion through doing.* This is to the essence of *EnlightenUp.* It's an understanding that there is nowhere to go, nothing to do, nobody you have to be except who you are right now. It is the inward journey that reflects living a life of spiritual elegance while seeking personal freedom toward renewed transformation and spirituality.

QUESTIONS TO PONDER:
- ♦ *As I use my spirituality to heighten my humanness, how can I use these resources to teach, support, and guide me on my path to EnlightenUp?*

♦ *How will my new learnings affect my relationship with myself and others?*
♦ *What have I learned about myself?*

EXERCISE:

As we have progressed from the basic understanding that our conditioned human belief system presents opportunities for growth, let's take a moment to consider how our spiritual belief system fosters a greater sense of conscious awareness. The following exercises will help you understand how the power of your beliefs relates to the choices you make and the effect those choices have on the direction and quality of your life. To exemplify this, I will use three scenarios: a divorce, a life threatening illness, and death.

PART ONE:
1. Define a situation. *For the sake of this exercise, let's use a divorce situation. In a divorce situation, extended family members will usually align their loyalties with the member of their own family, rather than that of the ex-spouse.*
2. Identify the human belief. *"When Joe and Mary got divorced, it was sad, but Joe wasn't a very good husband. We don't want to have anything to do with him. Mary deserves better, and we need to show our allegiance to Mary only."*
3. Identify the spiritual belief. *"When Joe and Mary got divorced, we felt sad for them and the children. We also understood that they each had their own issues to resolve and that it is inappropriate for us to side with one over the other. We will show our love and support in an open, loving, and supportive way to both of them."*
4. What are your choices? *Choices show us the workings of "cause and effect" in terms of the progression of events. Knowing what the possible consequences are, proceed to ask yourself: "What choice is proactive or reactive?" Notice the effects of these choice.*

In the above exercise, our spiritual path takes us on a journey whereby we learn lessons of strength, courage, discipline, as well as unconditional love, acceptance, and surrendering to what is in life and not what we expect. Unconditional love emanates from the acceptance that everyone is doing the best they can. Sometimes we are called to be together just as we are also called to divorce when the partnership is done.

Both beliefs express positive intentions of love; however, the human belief system reflects an enemy—fear—and prevents the believer from going beyond the scope of him or herself. On the other hand, the spiritual belief fosters a sense of love and understanding that goes beyond the scope of oneself and gives consideration to the "other."

PART TWO:

Now, let's expand on the exercise as we experience an added dimension of the process of choice:

1. Identify a problem in your life.
2. Identify your need.
3. Determine all your choices, listing all possibilities.
4. Determine the best one, let go of the situation without worry, and act on it.
5. If you encounter a situation you can't change, for example, a diagnosis of cancer, maintain your power without giving it to the cancer.
6. Determine what you are going to do. For example, with a diagnosis of cancer, accept it only after you have done everything you could do to get rid of it. Your choice is what you create in the moment, and the idea is to accept it for the moment. As you control it, you become the master of the situation because when life deals you an "effect," you are dealing with the cause.

PART THREE:

In some situations you have no choice. For example, death is inevitable. In this case you have no choice; therefore, you have no problem. Unless you decide to not like it or not want it, then that creates a problem for you. Since our expectations create the problem, we have a choice: either to hold on to the expectation or let it go.

Consider the element of fear as it finds its way into the equation. Fear leads us to make the wrong choices every time. In the face of fear, let's consider the following questions:

1. Decide who makes your choices for you. Is it you or another?
2. Will you give that power to another and live with the consequences? For example, if a doctor says you have a 20% chance of survival, will you allow that doctor to dictate the length of your existence?
3. What other choices do you have? You can choose to act in the way you want to act, feel, look, and believe. You can choose to let go of fear, hatred, unhappiness, and self-pity. You can choose the best in yourself and be your best. You can also choose to see the best in everyone else and see each person as a teacher instead of an enemy. Your choices become your reality.

SUMMARY:

Our beliefs direct us to create our own reality with the choices we make. The right choices that focus on love versus fear lead us to peace of mind, body, and heart. This equation of life fills us with peace, happiness, responsibility, and accountability for ourselves. Spiritual beliefs generate healthy choices that promote energy as we learn to respond appropriately with a sense of acceptance and surrender while maintaining our power.

The power of your beliefs enables you to make choices that create experiences, which become your reality. Allow yourself the chance to choose well and experience the opportunity of personal and spiritual satisfaction, fulfillment, and peace.

CHAPTER TWELVE

ENLIGHTENUP & EXPERIENCE
THE POWER
OF TRANSFORMATION

"May you live all the days of your life."
–Jonathan Swift

Transformation is about empowerment, enlightenment, and living a life of balance, harmony, peace, and joy. The inward journey represents a shift of going from the conditioned self to the true self.

As we come into our "own," we get in touch with our basic nature, which is connected to the various parts of ourselves, and we discover how to live a life of thoughtful action that promises balance, harmony, peace, and joy. Having integrity and feeling congruent with who we are without the stress that often accompanies the "conditioning" process of our culture paves the way for perfection.

Actress Sally Fields made a rather profound comment when she said, "I was raised to sense what someone wanted me to be, and I became that kind of person. It took me a long time not to judge myself through someone else's eyes." I find that statement to be admirable, self-assured, and an eloquent reflection of her own journey. It is important to never underestimate the courage and dedication it takes to overcome the forces of inner unrest. Those who are strong and enlightened are able to use their inner drive to provoke revolution and create the glory of evolution.

In light of the choices we make on our journey, let's take a moment to consider the following questions: How many people in our society live their lives driving others, drifting aimlessly, struggling at a frenetic pace, or allowing others to drive them? And, what is the attraction to the events and circumstances of

some of the daytime talk shows? The answer: Victimhood! No one wants to admit to being a victim (at least not consciously); however, every time we feel hurt, ignored, unseen, overlooked, or oppressed, we may very well be perceiving from a place of victim consciousness. Feeling out of balance with our life or out of control, weak, stressed, or disempowered may be signs that we are taking on the victim role.

Recall a situation where you felt rejected. Stay with that feeling. Where did you go with it? Most people feel sorry for themselves, and then they take it to a friend and share their story, only to receive sympathy. Is this a powerful way of living? No. While sympathy may help us get the attention we desire, it also makes us feel weak and angry. This anger then gets turned inward because we may begin to persecute and become the victimizer just as our predecessor had done to us. Welcome to the world of "victim consciousness." Unfortunately, it gets worse when there is a rescuer in sight.

What are the rescuers' motives? Even though they may have good intentions, they are obstacles to themselves and us. It is easy to get caught up in this endless progression of madness. The best strategy is to avoid the web of other people's "stuff" and beware of being roped into the role of victim, persecutor, or rescuer. It is unproductive to wallow in the wounds of others, and you are better off avoiding those situations at all costs. The key ingredient to stop this insanity is to practice the language strategies outlined in the preceding chapters and remember to focus on balance.

BALANCING ACTS

Balance is a delicate issue and a formidable challenge because we live in an environment of radical change. How we handle our lives in relationship to feeling a deep sense of inner peace has much to do with our ability to shift easily between rest and action. Other helpful measures include having a supportive network of friends, family, surroundings, and experiences that encourage us to deal confidently with hardship and the continuing internal and external paradoxes of life. The ability to set aside

162

personal concerns, observe without being judgmental, have faith in a greater power, and treat people with dignity, respect, love, and understanding gives us a renewed sense of balance.

These factors encourage us to learn how to take better care of others and ourselves, and are essential to maintaining quality in life and work. This multi-dimensional growth occurs when we stop conforming to the ways of this world and define and refine creative approaches to *EnlightenUp*.

As we grow through the dark experiences of others and ourselves and become more aligned with the Spirit, we continue to expand our perception of a different earthly role. Consider the possibility that it is not by chance that our world is a fertile ground for us to do our work and transform ourselves, while we continually learn how we shall all live together.

Mother Theresa's words capture and support the essence that our life's purpose is to learn, manifest our love, and leave our intended legacy. She wrote:

Life is an opportunity; benefit from it.
Life is beauty; admire it.
Life is bliss; taste it.
Life is a dream; realize it.
Life is a challenge; meet it.
Life is a duty; complete it.
Life is a game; play it.
Life is a promise; fulfill it.
Life is sorrow; overcome it.
Life is a song; sing it.
Life is a struggle; accept it.
Life is a tragedy; confront it.
Life is an adventure; dare it.
Life is luck; make it.
Life is too precious; do not destroy it.
Life is life; fight for it.

THE TRANSFORMATIONAL PROCESS

Using the model below, let's discuss the meaning of this transformational process and how it all fits together as it relates to

163

how we live our lives. As I see it, as you Live In Fulfillment Every day, the more enlightened you become or are. Essentially, you **live, learn, love,** and leave a **legacy**.

Steven Covey talks about the dimensions of ourselves: to live, learn, love, and leave a legacy. I see a correlation of how these aspects relate to parts of ourselves from a physical, intellectual, social/emotional/psychological, and spiritual perspective. I also see a correlation of how these parts connect with living a life of thoughtful action. In essence, it is this last part that provides clues for us on how to be spiritual in a secular society.

When we **live,** we usually focus on issues involving economic security and survival, which are connected to the physical nature of ourselves. We must give our bodies the proper rest and exercise to ensure health, security, and survival. We do this by living a life of thoughtful action, whereby we define and articulate our needs, establish boundaries, and develop strategies to deal with both the joys and complexities of life.

As we live our lives in this way, we **learn** how to make this happen. Learning is another dimension of our nature. When we learn, we develop the intellectual, mental part of ourselves that focuses on self-development and fulfillment. This illuminating experience of self-knowledge awakens us and enables us to live a life of thoughtful action. Stillness, solitude, and reflection are the necessary ingredients for the mind to develop a sense of awareness and consciousness that enables us to go beyond self and be the best we can be.

In order to fulfill the learning aspect of our nature, we need to utilize the adaptive part—the ability to **love**. To love is to engage in the social, emotional, psychological part of others and ourselves. It is about relating with kindness and respect. Love is the "heart" aspect of our nature that requires intimacy. As we live a life of thoughtful action, we learn that disagreements are part of relationships. This "illumination" enables us to learn about diversity through listening and understanding, respecting, and having the skills to confront and transform the relationship to a new level. Knowing who you are and having the ability to love yourself is crucial to learning to love, understand, and respect another. Then and only then are we in a position to give and share our **legacy**.

When we impart our gifts to the world, we add a unique value that reflects and expands a renewed dimension of ourselves. This becomes a vital component of making our lives a masterpiece.

Have you ever thought about what happens when we die? If you believe that our bodies go back to the earth and our spirits or souls go to heaven, then we must wonder what happens to our intellect. There are people who believe that our intellect is imparted to those whose lives we have touched and the lives that they will in turn touch. It's a geometric progression. Therefore, to make this world a better place, we must live to the fullest and learn all that we can. In this way our **legacy** is truly connected to the spiritual part of us, which is about understanding, being, and contribution. It is this spiritual aspect that enables us to discover what it means to come from our truth or core selves with love. Our spirituality is also a place of invulnerability and openness, because when we are coming from love, we have humility, not fear. It is about being true with yourself and with others.

When this occurs in relationships, a renewed level of commitment and trust ensues. We feel a sense of caring coupled with a need to celebrate a special connection that has been born. This is a place where we can appreciate our families for the nurturing they provide us, and acknowledge our communities for the supportive ways in which we can express our creativity and grow through the connection of similar values and interests. This sacred ground enables us to experience and express healthy self-esteem, unique talents, qualities, abilities, and accomplishments. Both these places provide a unique sensation of beauty, rituals, traditions, and transcendence.

Take a moment to reflect and allow the words of this poem to resonate within you.

> *"For reasons we cannot know*
> *Happiness and inner peace*
> *Depend on our relationship*
> *To Beauty*
> *To Gratitude*
> *To Love*
> *And to the Service*
> *Of Something Greater*
> *Than the Self"*~Author Unknown

CREATE YOUR LIFE'S MASTERPIECE

If you were to express your feelings about life and humanity, would you say that we are all on this planet to engage in the process of creation? God needs us to be complete, and just as God or the Universe needs us, we need each other to complete the cycle and strive toward wholeness.

One day I came across a quote by John Gardner that was quite apropos to the message of this book. He said: "Human beings have always employed an enormous amount of clever devices for running away from themselves...we can keep ourselves busy, fill our lives with so many diversions, stuff our heads with so much knowledge, involve ourselves with so many people and cover so much ground that we never have time to probe the fearful and wonderful world within...By middle life, most of us are accomplished fugitives from ourselves." What a powerful and true statement.

In each and every one of us there is a formidable artist just waiting to be brought forth. We have a choice to reproduce our parents' story, leave the canvas blank, or recognize our own true identity and create a masterpiece of our own. Your life is yours to have and to hold. It is a gift that rests in your hands, and what you do with it is your choice. Emile Zola summed it up perfectly by stating: "The artist is nothing without gift, but gift is nothing without work."

As we experience the purification rituals in the second part of our life and leave behind the vestiges of the past, we open ourselves to a new life of freedom and pure potential. Making this a reality requires focused, intelligent, and diligent effort toward a learning process that bears no right or wrong. The process of *EnlightenUp* encourages the exploration of "Light Thinking" and experiences such as feedback as opposed to failure, lessons as opposed to mistakes, and choices as opposed to decisions.

YOUR LIFE IS YOUR CHOICE

Choices enable us to speak from the heart. They are intuitive insights rather than reasoned judgments. The famous twentieth century French artist, Marc Chagall, artfully expressed the language of the heart when he said, "If you create from the heart, nearly everything works; if from the head, almost nothing." As we become more enlightened through our experiences, we learn and develop a greater sense of consciousness. Then the constant need for intense "decision making," which can take endless effort, decreases as our foundation becomes stronger. Now when opportunities present themselves, we can confidently open ourselves to the choices offered, knowing that in the end those choices will be good and right. Initially, we often question the process; however, trusting and surrendering show us endless possibilities that shine light at the end of the tunnel. Feeling the evolutionary synchronicity allows us to sense when the extraordinary becomes the ordinary.

Here's an example of this process. When my husband and I were looking for a used car for our daughter, we found the perfect car; however, it was not the bargain we hoped to find. As the Universe would have it, the car was pristine and perfect in every way but the price. In addition, our daughter already had a car, and we didn't want to be stuck with an additional vehicle. We bargained for as low as we could, looked at one another, and finally chose to think about it.

As we were driving away, my husband said he wasn't sure what to do next. I commented that at that moment neither

one of us had to know, and that after our discussion of the pros and cons, it clearly was time for silence. During those moments he proceeded to call his office and received a message from someone who was interested in buying the car we wanted to replace. We laughed at the slim chance of that happening as well as at how the buyer was able to get his office number.

That experience was an enigma and another example of how effortless choices can sometimes be. Choices happen at the perfect time and place. For us, there was no question that the choice to purchase and sell the car had been made for us.

LEARN FROM LIFE'S PARADOXES

The paradoxes of life require us to observe and learn. When we understand some of their subtleties, we can actually find some humor to the process and not take life so seriously. For example, the comedian George Carlin writes, "The paradox of our time in history is that we have taller buildings but shorter tempers, wider freeways, but narrower viewpoints. We spend more, but have less. We buy more, but enjoy less. We have bigger houses and smaller families, more conveniences, but less time." And so the parallels continue as we have learned to rush, but not to wait, have higher incomes, but lower morals, more food, but less appeasement, more acquaintances, but fewer friends. These are all true and pressing issues. Yet when we observe them closer, we can see the humor as well as the frustration these paradoxes present. That's the level at which you want to be able to observe events.

Recognizing paradoxes and making choices are part of our creation process. Therefore, it is not alien that we continue to attract relationships in our lives that are for the ultimate purpose of our continuing personal growth. The missing elements in our own growth and development that create longings are the ones we unconsciously strive to satisfy in relationships with our beloved. To illustrate this point, consider the story of Betty Ford.

Betty's father traveled extensively, and as a result, Betty vowed that she would never marry anyone like him. Having a husband at home was an important criterion for her, and when she married Gerald Ford, she believed he would fulfill that need. However, with the unanticipated turn of political events that precipitated in both their lives, Betty found herself and her four children alone. What a terrifying experience this must have been for her, yet it is often that which we are most fearful of that we attract. So perhaps Gerald Ford was both an obstacle and conduit who served a greater purpose in her life in order for her to deal with her unfulfilled longings and to heal and emancipate herself from her own fears.

As a result of her painful ordeal, Betty had a nervous breakdown. In addition, she was dealing with arthritis and a pinched nerve in her neck, which necessitated the use of drugs. This situation, coupled with the intense emotional pain of separation, became a burden too great for Betty to deal with. Alcohol became her only escape. Unfortunately, her addictions grew worse and progressed to the point where her life was threatened. Her family gathered together and decided something had to be done. With their support and the institutionalized care that Betty received, she was able to heal.

While she was First Lady, Betty realized the impact of her power upon the country and clearly used her unique position to empower others. She supported equal rights for women, and when she was diagnosed with cancer, Betty was another example of awareness and support. Her drug and alcohol addiction was pivotal in the opening of The Betty Ford Center for treatment, which has treated over 50,000 patients. No words can ever describe the depth of this woman who is a shining example of strength, courage, fortitude, and compassion.

The purpose of this story is to illustrate the message that "we will be attracted to someone who will be the answer to our issues provided we are committed to doing our work." The irony is that the other person will not necessarily fulfill our longings. This is an illusion, and it is often the person we are drawn to that becomes the one in which we need to work out our perceptions with. Consider it an opportunity to construct yourself and grow even though there are times when people tend to lose themselves in the process and become intertwined

with the "other" self. This paradox has a life and energy of its own—one that is already predetermined in some way and yet presents itself with choices.

William Jennings Bryan is known to have said, "Destiny is not a matter of chance; it is a matter of choice. It is not something to be waited for, but rather something to be achieved." Yes, this language is paradoxical, and to refute or explain it is futile because the language of the Gods speaks for itself. It's no different than when we feverishly work to create and achieve our potential, and no matter what happens we just can't seem to get past "go." Since the timing of events is often outside our control, it behooves us to use this time wisely as we reflect and ask, "What am I feeling?" "What is it I need to learn?" "What are the lessons I need to experience and grow from? Is it Patience? Perseverance? Endurance? Courage? Understanding? Compassion? Forgiveness? Love? and/or Acceptance?" Then, ask for the grace to get through the situation and do the best you can.

Remember the only things we are in charge of are the elements of what we believe, the ideas we hold to be spiritually true, our emotions, our attitudes, and where and how we spend our energy. Have faith as you encounter difficult times and know that living through those disempowering experiences are the pathways in which to become increasingly brave, enlightened, and empowered. At the same time it is useless to be afraid that we are less than perfect, because it is this fragile thread that binds us together in order for us to grow and do our work.

COMING FULL CIRCLE

Our experiences are symbolic to the flow of life. The symbols of death and rebirth manifest themselves over and over again in our everyday life, not only within the cells of our bodies, but also in the events that occur throughout our existence.

People with a strong personal foundation center their lives on learning from the past, living in the present, and working and planning toward the future. Being in the flow and feeling a sense of integrity with who you are means having no overwhelming concerns or regrets and putting your energy into resourceful states. Wherever you place your attention, therein also lies your intention. We all possess the power to bring these intentions into our life.

This type of thinking defies the reactive model that drains our energy. It is a different mindset that enables us to feel alignment with our mission, passion, creativity, fulfillment, balance, growth, and harmony as we live and breathe each and every day. This sense of "integrity" or knowing promotes a sense of awareness as to how special, unique, and precious we are. Shakespeare said it so well: "To thine own self be true, and thou canst not be false to any man (or woman)."

Before I close, allow me to share some of the beautiful moments of life that make it so precious, worthwhile, and rewarding;

- Take time to dream. It is a soulful experience that allows you to reach for the stars.

- Take time to think because it is the source of power, growth, and enlightenment.

- Take time to learn because knowledge is power.

- Take time to work and play hard. Work gives you a strong sense of purpose and enables you to achieve success and fulfill your dreams. Play is the secret of youth. This unique blend promotes well being.

- Take time to worship in whatever manner you choose because this expression of your spirituality gives sacredness to a mundane world.

- Take time to laugh and experience "internal jogging" because it helps with life's "stuff."

- Take time for health because it is one of the truest treasures of life.

- Take time for friends and family because they are the "jewels and treasures to behold." They are your truest wealth.

- Take time to love because it is a gift we give to others and to ourselves, and it is a source of joy, peace, harmony, and contentment.

Above all else, always remember that you are your biggest asset. Invest in yourself and go the extra mile. In so doing know that whatever you sow you will reap, for every gardener knows that after the digging, planting, and the long season of tending and growing, the harvest comes.

CHAPTER THIRTEEN

LET'S
PULL IT TOGETHER
"TOGETHER"

"When you're ready to exchange your illusions for reality, when you're ready to exchange your dreams for facts, that's the way you find it all. That's where life finally becomes meaningful. Life becomes beautiful."–Anthony de Mello

We are living in a time where change is happening so rapidly that it is difficult to make organization of it all. The window of opportunity to seize what we want is shrinking, and in order to achieve all our goals, we need to challenge those beliefs we had come to know as absolutes. Being able to think about today and thrust forward is a necessity to survival and to the cultivation of a leadership style that enables us to empower others and ourselves. In so doing, we will individually and collectively create a community of cooperation, commitment, purpose, and trust.

The single most important ingredient of successful people is their ability to effectively interact, behave, and communicate with others. Whenever we have personal, professional, or organizational change, we need to start with our individual understanding, growth, and development and work outward, whether it be at work or home. The bottom line is about accountability and responsibility, very much in line with Gandhi's advise to leaders, "You must become the change you want to see in the world."

Change occurs both on an internal and external level. While we have no control over the external environment, we do have control over our actions. Let's take a look at the following Transformational Change Cycle. While reading it, be mindful of Thomas Edison's expression, "Restlessness is discontent, and discontent is the first necessity."

The cycle comprises the following four stages of awareness:
1. Initiation Phase, where we feel dissatisfaction and a need for changing values and visions. This tension for change creates the desire for change.
2. Uncertainty Phase, where we experiment, take some risks, and experience confusion and ambiguity.
3. Transformational Phase, where the creative breakthrough appears. It's the "Ah-Ha" that serves to reframe situations.
4. Competence or Excellence Phase, which leads to mastery as a result of completions.

You may already be aware that you are in different places within this cycle in various areas in your life, and so these stages are normal and for our highest good. Understanding where you are in each phase will be useful in developing clarity toward making more appropriate choices that affect your life journey.

OUR PURPOSE TOGETHER

My goal throughout this book has been to encourage and support you as you develop a greater understanding and appreciation of yourself and others, and to teach you new ways to adapt. Why? Because the key to your effectiveness in life is linked to your ability to communicate appropriately while understanding and meeting the needs of a majority of people.

Knowing that your values determine the drivers in your life, which in turn stimulate and drive your behaviors, you can immediately use this information to determine if those behaviors are getting you the results you want. For example, have you ever walked into a store and been turned off by a salesperson? Do you think it was the person's intention to turn you away? Probably not. However, it does happen because most people are inclined to sell the way they buy.

By now you are aware that people possess different communication styles. Some open the door to communication while others slam it shut. Different styles can create feelings of judg-

174

ment. These are the workings of the mind that prevent us from appreciating others. This concept enables us to understand and accept other people for who they are and know that they are doing the best they can.

Fortunately, behavioral styles can change. Values and belief systems, however, are a bit more difficult to alter. Since belief systems cause expectations, which create attitudes and drive behaviors, let's start with the Key to Awareness. This key will enable us to get a "check up from the neck up" by discovering attitudes and expectations that may or may not cause stress in our lives.

First, let's create a level of understanding that there is no right or wrong. It is about identifying patterns, beliefs, and determining our needs as well as the needs of others. When we are able to understand ourselves and appreciate others, we find ways to adapt and meet the majority of peoples' needs. Along the way we will be able to identify strengths and changes most important to improving effectiveness. You will also be able to develop strategies that include setting boundaries that will serve to protect you and provide you with a safe place to grow as you learn how to discern one situation from another. All in all, these efforts will support your commitment to go forward.

The topics we will cover are Suppositions, Language and Beliefs, Affirmations, Pathways to EnlightenUp, and "Artful" Strategies.

1. Suppositions will serve to open our perspective and create a basis for an objective reality in lieu of a subjective one.
2. Language and beliefs are the spiritual paradoxes that enable us to make better choices and give greater meaning and direction to our humanity.
3. Pathways to EnlightenUp are growthful moments that explain the feelings of going from being conditioned to becoming more congruent and free.
4. Affirmations support, encourage, and validate a new direction that promotes future potential.
5. "Artful" Strategies provide the questions that pave the way toward clarity, awareness, and action.

SUPPOSITIONS

What would happen if you believed in one or more or all of the following suppositions? As you read them, determine the ones that sound true for you. Then, as you begin to adopt them, notice how your perceptions begin to change and how those changed perceptions affect your life.

- Everyone has the resources he or she needs.
- The worth of an individual is constant, while behavior can change.
- The map is not the territory. As we respond to our "subjective" reality instead of an "objective" more secular reality, be mindful that 97 percent of what we project is our reality while we only let in 2 to 3 percent of the other person.
- It is better to have choices than not to have choices.
- Behavioral flexibility is more useful than having limited behavioral choices.
- Every behavior has a positive intention.
- There are no mistakes, only feedback.

As you continue to read, absorb, and digest the above suppositions, you can see, hear, and feel yourself changing.

LANGUAGE & BELIEF SYSTEMS

Now, let's take a look at the following language and beliefs that support the spiritual part of us as we learn to use them to overcome the challenges of our own human frailties. The following is a list of possible beliefs that will enable you to reap enormous benefits. Be mindful that you are in control. Only you know what is right for you and what specifically sounds true. However, also remember that as you continue to change, you will create and adopt other beliefs that may not have been previously appropriate. This is truly an opportunity to use the spiritual language you have learned and design your own customized belief system that will meet your physical, intellectual, and spiritual needs.

- I am worthy, deserving, and loved. (This belief is amazing because if we only knew that we are special and were born

this way, we wouldn't have to work so hard all our lives proving it.)
- I belong and am connected to the Universal Spirit.
- People behave and communicate in a style of their own, and everyone is doing the best they can. (Note: According to Einstein, two things are universal: 1) human stupidity, and 2) the earth is round. Einstein also mentions that coincidence is God's way of remaining anonymous.)
- We are given the seeds or circumstances we require for our own awakening and depending upon how we plant them or interpret them determines how we grow.
- People can be conduits or obstacles or both.
- Our most trying experiences in life are our most growthful ones.
- We need to experience the darkness before the lightness.
- Everything happens for a reason, and for some things there are no reasons, especially when we enter the multisensorial domain that extends beyond our five senses.
- I have control over my actions and not the actions of others. (Note: Change is both internal and external. We have control over internal changes [ourselves], not external [others]. In addition, remember that we did not cause or create others.)
- Power and control can be abusive and manipulative when they are used over others.
- We have power within and over ourselves. When we give away that power we become enslaved or entrained.
- Power and control are best utilized within yourself. You can then help others empower themselves in their own way without attaching yourself to the outcome.
- Freedom is having and maintaining that power within and using it to promote your growth and potential.
- It is stupid not to forgive and forget; naïve to forgive and forget; wise to forgive and not forget. Forgiveness is freeing oneself. (Note: Not forgetting allows us to feel when an event is being repeated. We can then change the situation by setting necessary boundaries for us to grow and move forward

within ourselves and in the relationship.)

- As you identify tolerations and define boundaries, it is important to identify where your energy is going.
- Everyone has his or her own life message. For the most part, the message is evolutionary as it unfolds and gets defined and refined in the process.
- Focus on the journey, not the end result. While life is a process, be mindful of living in the present. It is a gift.
- The heart knows the answers and has its reasons for which reason sometimes has no logic. The mind works as a great equalizer with the necessary questions.
- Life is not about what you expect rather than what it expects of you. It is an ongoing interaction between human will and Divine Providence.
- Happiness is the internal bliss that supports and understands not what you want, but what you get.
- Perfection is when you look back on your life.
- Surrender, acceptance, forgiveness, gratitude, love, and hope represent the mystery of faith that fosters accountability, centeredness, belongingness, freedom, and the experience of being alive.
- Spirituality gives sacredness to a mundane life: Belief (I can); Intentions (I want, I'm going); Commitment (I will, I have to).
- Platinum versus Golden Rule: Seek first to listen and understand. Then, be understood. What an opportunity to step outside and experience the territory.
- Compassion enables us to use our hearts when it comes to others while using our minds to question ourselves.
- Wherever great love exists, miracles happen.

As you develop a language and belief system designed to support your growth, notice the opportunities that exist for you on a grand scale. We know that when we change our beliefs, our expectations and attitudes change as well. The mys-

teries of faith and the wonders of being alive allow us to begin
to make a difference in this world. The beginnings of positive
thoughts, words, and behaviors will make the world a better
place.

AFFIRMATIONS

Affirmations support and nurture our growth. They are energetic conduits that represent pure potential and lead us toward
positive directions. Consider incorporating the following
affirmations into your life:

- I love and approve of myself because I am loving and lov-
able.
- As I move forward with joy and ease in my life, I feel balanced and fulfilled.
- Everything happens in the perfect time and space sequence. I
release the struggle of trying to make things happen.
- All is well in my world. I trust the Universe will take me
where I need to go, and wherever that is will be for my highest good and the common good of all.
- I am open to new ideas, insights, and knowledge so that I can
become more of who I am and less of who I am not.
- I will always maintain a healthy body, mind, and spirit. Every day in every way I am getting better, better, and better.
- I choose to trust while "letting go and letting God."
- I am always safe. The Universe protects me. My life and
actions are divinely guided. I grow in peace, love, and security every moment.

These affirmations serve to mobilize and focus you in the directions you need to go. Putting the intention out there, believing
it, and knowing it will evolve allows you to comfortably swim
in both chartered and unchartered waters. As you select the
affirmations that are appropriate for you and create new ones
along the way, allow yourself to experience all the joy, peace,
and inspirational healing of being one with the Universal Spirit.

These are the ways of those who journey toward securing the hopes and dreams of today and tomorrow.

Pathways to EnlightenUp

Pathways serve as conduits to support the evolution from slavery, entrainment, and conditioning to mental, physical, spiritual congruity and freedom. Jesus said, "You are the Light of the World." Whenever we experience a feeling of confusion or of being overwhelmed, pathways of "Light Thinking" serve to remind us of our light and guide us along the way. Allow the terminology to create a sense of renewed awareness that will pave the way toward your desired outcome.

- Are you feeling enslaved and entrained? This feeling, based in fear and control, is about relinquishing your power and handing it over to another.

- Are you feeling lost and questioning where and how you fit in? With awareness we metaphorically fall out of alignment with other planets and feel alien. As we wonder where we fit in, we enter the dark night of the soul to explore feelings, examine beliefs, question them, and create ones that support a new found freedom toward unlimited potential. Hope, faith, trust, courage, perseverance, and a sense of knowing that it will all be perfect in the end promotes mental, physical, and spiritual growth, freedom, and fulfillment. Be mindful that faith can keep hope afloat provided you hook into it. In troubled waters or the unknown there is nothing left but faith. This is the time to call upon your resourceful spiritual powers to take you where you need to go.

- Are you feeling pain or pleasure in your life? Pain motivates us to find our own individuality and uniqueness in self—the life force within us that is found in our hearts. We need to open up in order to heal. Healing does not precede opening up. They both occur simultaneously, and strength, courage, and trust are requirements.

- Are you feeling obstacles stemming from old belief patterns that inhibit potential growth and freedom? Confront the old belief patterns that impede your progress. Knowingness and mindfulness are the resources we have available for us to grow. Intuition and instinct are a dynamic combination, and they present themselves with the asking. Seek and you shall find; knock and the door shall open; ask and you will receive.

- How do we discover freedom? We discover freedom by opening up our hearts in two ways:

  1) Through the use of suggestive Suppositions, Language, and Affirmations.

  2) By using our minds to align ourselves and our hearts to open to others.

As you encounter transformational situations in your life, you will have to address some of the above questions. These feelings are normal and are part of the ongoing challenge as you learn to cohesively integrate your mind, body, and spirit toward a new level of awareness.

THE ART OF ENLIGHTEN UP

"What lies behind us and what lies before us are tiny matters compared to what lies within us." –Ralph Waldo Emerson

E ach of the strategies are part of your tool kit for success. They are the "artful" mechanics that teach us what we need to know in order to be more effective in our dealings with self and others. These models are purposefully designed to give you the necessary structure and support as you develop inner strength.

Let's take a look at a specific situation and see how various "strategic arts" can help us learn how to specifically focus on certain issues, take action, and respond appropriately.

SITUATION:

If an individual has a verbal and demonstrative communication style and finds him or herself in the presence of a significant other who is nondemonstrative by nature, he/she may tend to feel shut out, scared, sad, hurt, and angry.

THE ART OF SELF-AWARENESS

- Identify the issue and to whom it belongs. Remember, you only have control over your actions. You cannot control, create, or cause the other person.
- Be mindful and observe without the impulse to mind read, judge, or blame.
- Take time out, remember to breathe, and restore to get clarity.
- Consider the two entities of the ego and heart. The conditioned self comes from the ego, and the true self comes from

the heart. The task is to discover and uncover the layers of beliefs that don't work and create new beliefs that serve to energize as well as help you achieve your potential.

Sample Ego Belief: "My partner SHOULD openly communicate with me at all time."

THE ART OF SELF-QUESTIONING
In relation to the above example, you would next ask yourself the following questions:
- What happens when I believe this way?
- What do I achieve when I believe this way?
- How much energy am I using to finance this belief?
- Where in my body do I feel the drain from this negative energy?
- Does this belief serve me?
- Do I have to have my partner be demonstrative to know that I am loved, deserving, worthy, and connected?
- How would it look, feel, or sound to have a different belief that is more congruent with my true self that supports new change and growth?
- What is stopping me?
- What do I have to do to make this change?
- How will I do it in terms of utilizing internal and external resources?
- When will I do it?

THE ART OF PURPOSEFULNESS AWARENESS
Remember that relationships are an opportunity to grow. We need the other person in our lives so that we can consciously identify our shadow side through these emotional upsets, discover effective ways to transform it, and help each other achieve his or her potential.

THE ART OF IDENTIFYING NEEDS AND WANTS

To better understand yourself, think about the following possibilities:

- I need time for family, my work, play, community, and myself.
- I need a sense of purpose.
- I need love, appreciation, respect, and validation.
- I want to feel a sense of belonging and connectedness.
- I want to feel worthy.
- I want to feel love, appreciation, respect, and validation.
- In essence, I need and want to feel heard and seen.

This is a time for you to be ruthlessly honest with yourself. It is important to identify individual needs and wants just as it is important to identify those in a relationship. Confusing the two can drain the relationship. It is vital that we restore ourselves in order to fulfill our own needs as well as work together to fulfill relationship needs.

THE ART OF EFFECTIVE COMMUNICATION "DO'S"
Do:

- Listen: hear in both a passive and active manner
- Acknowledge: clarify, paraphrase, give feedback, and summarize
- Explore Options: elicit possibilities, resources, and actions
- Offer Advice: share your point of view

THE ART OF EFFECTIVE COMMUNICATION "DON'TS"
Don't:

- Attack, blame, defend, criticize, complain, condemn
- Rescue, fix, control
- Assume other's responsibilities
- Give unsolicited advice

THE ART OF EFFECTIVE DIALOGUE

Remember to always speak in "I" language. For example, "When we have a conversation and you shut down, I feel shut out, scared, and angry because I care about you and believe it is important for partners to openly communicate so that we can better understand each other and help each other achieve a greater potential."

THE BEAUTY OF THE "ARTS"

The "Arts" are effective solutions to challenges that help us get to the core of issues, suggest appropriate remedies, and sustain us with the ongoing wisdom of life. They can be a continuing source of inspiration as we deal with the day-to-day complexities of life and emerge with a renewed sense of resilience.

You can utilize these "arts" to learn, grow, define, and refine your character while you continue to seek new beliefs, expectations, and attitudes. As you experience *EnlightenUp* and see, hear, and feel yourself deeply and intensely alive, pay attention to the voice inside that speaks, "This is the real me!"

It is my hope that the journey we have embarked on together will make the difference you want in your life. Broadening your perspectives, creating new beliefs, cultivating a new language, and learning "artful strategies" in which to take responsibility enables you to create your life masterpiece—one that is deserving of your uniqueness, beauty, and strength. What greater gift to give others and yourself than the gift of who you truly are. May your continuing journey be a wondrous and sincere expression of the creative process of life and the heartfelt love and joys I wish for you.

PEACE & HAPPINESS ALWAYS.

SUGGESTED READINGS AND REFERENCES

EnlightenUp is a result of ideas, thoughts, and suggestions from many sources, including lectures, interviews, articles, and stimulating conversations. There are a few resources that I would like to specifically cite for their rich content.

Berends, Polly Berrien. *Coming To Life*
     (New York: Harper & Row, 1990).
Bonnstetter, Bill J., Judy I. Suiter, and Randy Widrick.
     The Universal Language of DISC: A Reference Manual
     (Scottsdale, AZ: Target Training International, 1993).
Borysenko, Joan. *Minding the Body, Mending The Mind*
     (New York: Bantam New Age Books, 1987).
Borysenko, Joan. *The Power Of The Mind To Heal*
     (Niles, Illinois: Nightingale Conant, 1993).
Chopra, Deepak. *Magical Mind Magical Body*
     (Niles, Illinois: Nightingale Conant, 1990).
Chopra, Deepak. *How To Know God*
     (New York: Harmony Books, 2000).
Covey, Stephen. *The 7 Habits of Highly Effective People*
     (New York: Fireside, 1990).
Dilts, Robert B. *Visionary Leadership Skills*
     (Capitola, California: Meta Publications, 1996).
Hay, Louise L. *Heal Your Body*
     (Carlsbad, California: Hay House, Inc., 1982, 1984).
May, M.D., Gerald G. *Addiction & Grace*
     (San Francisco: Harper & Row, 1988).
Moore Thomas, *Care of the Soul*
     (New York: Harper Collins, 1992).
Moore Thomas, *Soul Mates*
     (New York: Harper Collins, 1994).
Moore, Thomas, *The Art of Soul Work*
     (Hay House: New Dimensions, 1997).
Myss, Caroline. *Energy Anatomy*
     (Louisville, Colorado: Sounds True, 1996).

Myss, Caroline. *Why People Don't Heal*
(Louisville, Colorado: Sounds True, 1994).
Myss, Caroline. *Archetypes*
(Indianapolis, IN: Great Lakes Training
Associates, Inc., 1997).
Nouwen, Henri J. M. *Life Of The Beloved*
(New York: Crossroad, 1992).
Nouwen, Henri J.M. *The Return Of The Prodigal Son*
(New York: Image, Doubleday, 1994).
Robbins, Anthony. *Personal Power*
(San Diego, California: Guthy –Renker Corporation,
1993).
Ruiz, Don Miguel. *The Four Agreements*
(San Rafael, California: Amber-Allen).
Walsch, Neale Donald. *Conversations with God:
an Uncommon Dialogue*
(New York:G. P. Putnam's Sons).
Stuart Wilde, *Infinite Self*
(Niles, Illinois: Nightingale Conant, 1995).
Zukav, Gary. *The Seat Of The Soul*
(New York: Fireside, 1990).

Take The Next Step

"*EnlightenUp* is a heartfelt, genuine, and affirming book that explores fascinating pathways toward spiritual fulfillment. The generosity of spirit and deeply felt optimism that radiates from her book is proof that her prescriptions for becoming a happier, more involved human being do actually work." –Melinda Camber Porter, artist, filmmaker, and author of *Badlands*

Check with your leading bookstore or order here.
Toll-Free: 1-866-37-CAMEO

$\mathcal{ENLIGHTEN}\mathcal{UP}$ **$15.95**

Freeing The Real You!   x quantity _____

ISBN #0-9715739-2-1   + shipping _____

+ sales tax _____

Shipping
USA: $4.95 for first book; add $2.00 for each additional book
Canada: $6.00 for first book; add $4.00 for each additional book

Order Total [   ]

credit card # _____expires_____

please sign _____

Paying by ___Check* ___VISA ___ MasterCard **No CODs**
* Mail to: Cameo Publications
            PO Box 8006, Hilton Head Island 29938
For Faster Service FAX Orders To: 843-785-8722

Please Print

Name _____

Address _____

City/State/Zip_____Country_____

Phone ( )_____Email(optional) _____